BROKEN SILENCE SERIES

Was It Worth It?

A Journey of Leaving, Losing, and Becoming

BROKEN SILENCE SERIES

Was It Worth It?

A Journey of Leaving, Losing, and Becoming

MARYAM RAFIEE

ADAM BRAVER, SERIES EDITOR

FAHIMEH AMIRMAHANI, EMMA HANSEN, AND AUDREY RYAN, EDITORIAL ASSISTANTS

UNIVERSITY OF NEW ORLEANS PRESS

Was It Worth It?: A Journey of Leaving, Losing, and Becoming
by Maryam Rafiee
Adam Braver, Series Editor
Broken Silence Series

First Edition
Printed in the United States of America
Printed on acid-free paper

Book design by Kevin Stone
Cover design by Kevin Stone

Fahimeh Amirmahani, Emma Hansen, and Audrey Ryan, Editorial Assistants

ISBN: 978-1-60801-477-4

University of New Orleans Press
2000 Lakeshore Drive
New Orleans, Louisiana 70148
unopress.org

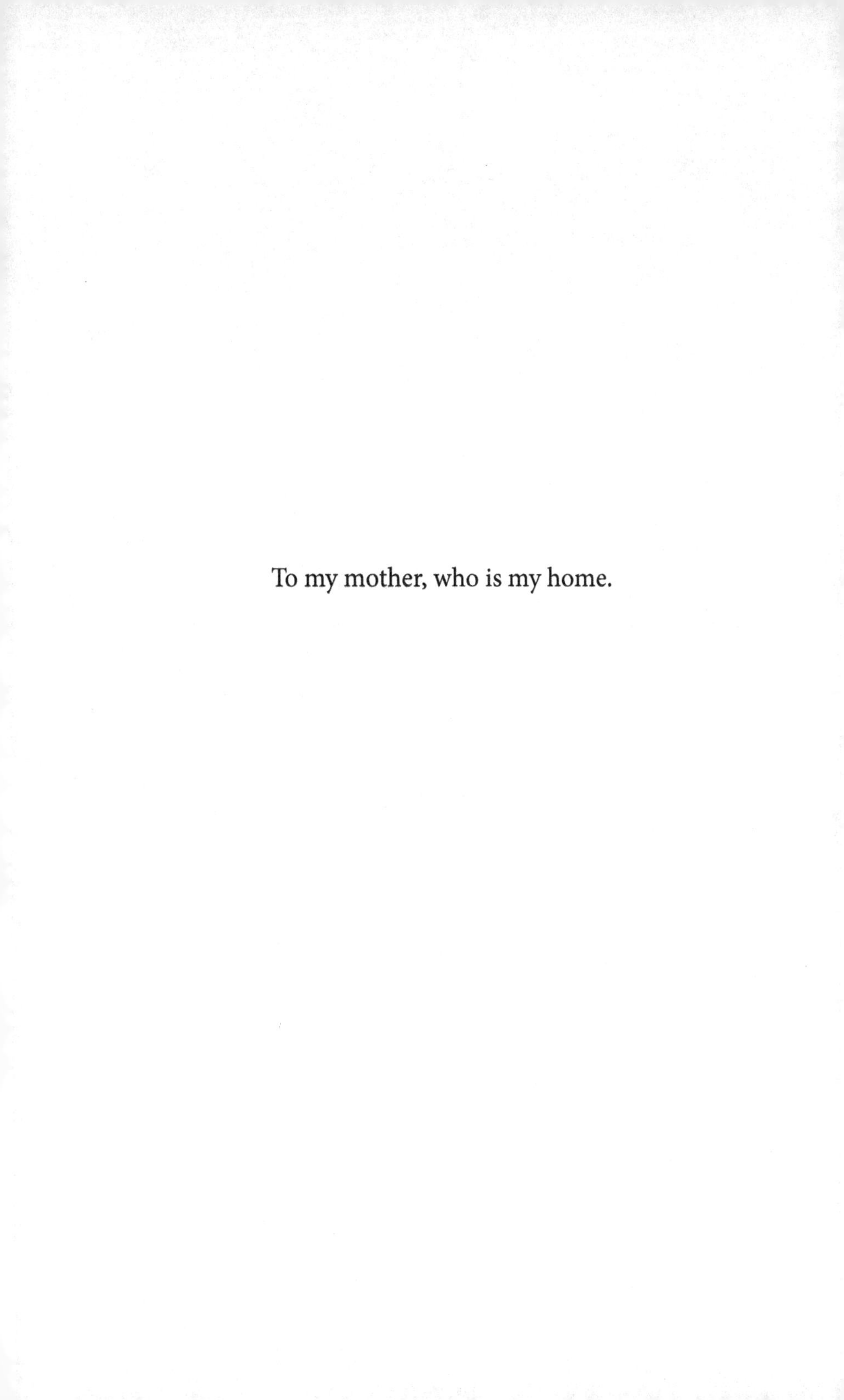

To my mother, who is my home.

EDITORS NOTE

In 2018, Maryam Rafiee published her first book, *Dear Baba.* At the time of publication, her father, Professor Mohammad Hussien Rafiee, an academic, scientist, and political prisoner had recently been released from what was widely understood to be an arbitrary detention in Iran's notorious Evin Prison. During the time of her father's imprisonment, Maryam, who had left Iran for the safety of Canada, began what would become a worldwide campaign on behalf of her father, joining efforts with Scholars at Risk, primarily through its Student Advocacy Seminar program, which trains and engages student advocates globally. Together, they would work to raise awareness about her father through media and public events, and seek to gain support from key decisionmakers, politicians, and everyday people.

It was during this period when Maryam revisited letters she had written as a teenager to her father when he first had been detained as a political prisoner. These letters became the basis of *Dear Baba*, an epistolary memoir that chronicled Maryam's coming of age in the aftermath of the Iranian Revolution, the growing understanding of her father and his principles, the appreciation for her mother's tenacity to see her husband freed, and just the sheer joy and confusion of teenage girlhood that transcended culture and politics.

But to see *Was It Worth It?* as a follow up or part two of *Dear Baba* would be a mistake. Although the chronology picks up after her father's release, this is a book of a different kind of politics: ones of migration, of displacement, and of identity. It is about reimagining, disappointment, outsiderness, loneliness, and a search for belonging.

The personal essays (or "stories," as Maryam calls them) that make this memoir focus on Maryam restarting her life in her new home of Canada, where principles of democracy are liberating but, for Maryam, not always welcoming. Throughout the narrative lies an ongoing tension between the cultural assumptions that undermine one's sense of value and dignity with a kind of visible-invisibility, and the idealism of hope and possibility.

But *Was it Worth It?* is not just a reflection on isolation and displacement, it also is a book about appreciating what one often forgets when in the moment, in this case, the joys Maryam had in her life in Iran. Rituals and family customs. Foods and activities. The appreciation of being among a shared spirit and home, one that had nothing to do with national and international politics.

Complicated? Complex? Of course. We live through times in which the predicate for power is based on separation and isolation. Where the individual and their dignity is dispensable for advancement of the larger goal. And yet, we also live in an era where on a personal level there still exists great mercy and tenderness and commitment for others. That is the challenge of *Was It Worth It?*, and what makes it so moving – asking the persistent and unanswerable question of if, in the end, the sacrifices of the battle are worth it.

I will end by thanking those who helped this process, from the team at UNO Press to the keen readership of Clare Robinson, Emma Hansen, Audrey Ryan, and Fahimeh Amirmahani. And of course, Maryam Rafiee, for writing such a candid and moving memoir that not only is her experience, but perhaps all of our experiences in one way or another.

–Adam Braver
Broken Silence Series Editor
Edgewood, Rhode Island
March 2026

THE RAID

I was struggling to be calm. I glanced at my husband. Aydin was trying to appear cool-headed, too, but the truth is, we both were stressed. We got our boarding passes and walked through the police check. I gently pushed Aydin to go first and followed behind him. He had promised that if something went wrong for me, he would leave Iran and go to Canada as planned. I wasn't sure he would keep his promise.

"Where are you going?" the agent asked, staring at Aydin without blinking.

"Canada," Aydin answered.

The agent held Aydin's passport open while he looked at his computer. After a moment that felt like ages, he stamped the passport. Then he raised his head to look at me. My heart was pounding in my throat.

Over the past week, I had imagined this moment a thousand times through different scenarios. In one, the agent would call someone, and in a few moments, an officer would come and escort me to a room. A higher-ranking officer would question me about where I was going. Then he would tell me that my passport was confiscated and that I was not allowed to leave the country until the matters with the security intelligence were settled. In a worst-case scenario, I imagined that I would be arrested at the airport and taken to prison.

I stared at the agent while replaying all these scenarios in mind. His lips were moving, but I couldn't hear what he was saying. The only sound I could hear was my heartbeat. I swallowed, trying to wet my throat, but a bitter taste left me feeling nauseous.

"Pardon?" I managed to say.

"What is the reason for your travel?" he asked again.

"Immigration," I answered.

He moved his hand toward the exit stamp and pressed it firmly on the last page of my passport. My breath hitched in my throat. I was frozen and didn't know what to do next. Aydin stretched his hand, grasped mine, and covered my trembling fingers.

Together, we walked in silence towards the security check. The terminal was nearly empty. Our flight was the last flight of the night. It seemed everyone had gone home except us, passengers of flight TK083.

The floor had just been mopped; all I could smell was bleach. My eyes and nose began to burn. I covered my nose with my scarf and quickened my steps. At the checkpoint, I left Aydin for the women's booth.

The woman agent touched my private parts. I cared less this time. Earlier, I would have reminded her to be respectful, but now, the only thing I could think of was to pass through this stage as well. I stood still and let her do whatever she wanted.

"Where is your money?" she asked.

I looked at her for the first time since stepping into the booth. She was overweight, with black tattooed eyebrows. I pointed to my passport bag.

"How much do you have?" she asked.

I followed her hands as they reached for my bag. The white cotton gloves she wore had turned gray from dirt.

"Three thousand dollars," I said.

She opened the bag and touched the money. "You can go," she said, returning my passport bag.

I stepped out of the women's booth.

Aydin waved me towards him. "Drink," he said, handing me a bottle of water. I could hardly swallow the first gulp before I started coughing. He gently tapped my back. "Drink more," he said.

"I can't." I handed back the bottle.

At the boarding lounge, we sat on a row of seats bolted to the floor. We exchanged no words. We had one hour until our flight departure, and I was trying to distract myself from thinking about what would happen next.

A woman was sitting opposite, bottle-feeding her baby. Her other child was asleep on the terminal seats, his head on her lap. *Are they also immigrating to Canada or just visiting? Where is the father? Maybe he's gone first to sort everything out, and now they are joining him. Perhaps they are one of those who decided to emigrate for their children's fortune.* Suddenly the woman dropped the milk bottle. Desperate, she turned around for help.

I should get up and give her the bottle, I told myself. But my body remained rigid. I turned my head away, avoiding eye contact with her.

My father's call brought me back to the moment. "Have you passed the police check?" he asked.

"Yes," I said.

It was after midnight. We knew that none of our family members would be sleeping. They were worried I would be detained and that I would not be allowed to leave the country.

"Call me before your flight departs," he said and hung up.

A week before, my life had changed forever. Now, I wasn't sure what was expected of me. I only wanted to board flight TK083 for Montreal to end this nightmare.

*

Summer is hot in Tehran, with scorching July days inching up to 39 or 40°C. I'd been out all day, checking off the list I had prepared for our move to Canada: the last dental checkup, buying essential items, translating the documents, and so on. There are so many things to do before departing. I was trying to get as much done as possible to spend more time at home with my parents during my last days in Iran. Aydin and I had decided to move back to our parents' homes for the final month before leaving Iran so we could create more memories with them.

It should have been routine, this checking-things-off-the-list, but I'd had a feeling that something bad would happen since the morning.

It was Ramadan. Although I wasn't fasting, I hadn't eaten or drunk all day.

"It's the heat and hunger," Aydin said when I shared my anxiety with him. "You'll feel better when you eat and rest at home."

I returned home at iftar time, the echo of prayers preceding the azan drifting from the nearby mosque. Knowing my father was fasting, I anticipated the table set for iftar. But as I stepped into my parental home, what awaited me was far from the usual.

My father was sitting on the couch in the living room, surrounded by ten intelligence agents. Their stubbly beards and untucked shirts served as their uniform. Before him, huge piles of books and papers, computer drives, and laptops cluttered the table and floor.

This was in 2014, at the height of Iran's nuclear negotiation with the world powers. Despite the dissatisfaction of the hardliners, the newly elected government was determined to resolve the nuclear issue. After years of tensions, when sanctions had crippled the economy, it seemed there was no choice but to negotiate. My father, a scholar and political activist, supported the diplomatic approach to resolving the nuclear problem. He believed an agreement would reduce the threat of another war in the Middle East and lead to finally easing economic sanctions.

He was giving speeches and writing about the benefits of an agreement that had infuriated the hardliners. They could not tolerate his activities. The raid on our home was to confiscate his writings to threaten him so he would not comment on political issues. In one word, to silence him.

"Baba, are you all right?" I managed to ask.

"Yes, hon. I am fine," he said in his usual calm tone, but there was something in the way he sat on the edge of the couch—hands locked on his lap, the forward tilt of torso and furrowed forehead—that I found worrisome.

"These men want me to sign a receipt for the things they are confiscating, but I won't sign unless they exclude your laptop." He pointed at my laptop on the table.

I squeezed through the circle of agents and, in a sudden movement, grabbed my laptop and pressed it to my chest. "No, no. This is mine. You don't have any right to take it," I said, stepping back out of the circle.

I had a few days left before I immigrated to Canada, and my thirty years of life were on that laptop. Photos, videos, diaries, articles, projects—anything that could be saved digitally, including personal things I did not want strangers to see. There was nothing on that laptop that mattered to the security of the country.

All of a sudden, I broke out in a cold sweat. *Where is my passport? What if they took that too?* I didn't say a word—I didn't want to draw attention. Instead, I waited for a moment of distraction. When they started asking questions of my father, I used the opportunity to run to my room. I found my passport there, resting on my desk. What a relief. I then hid it in the bottom of my luggage, lying open in the middle of the room.

"I will not let you ruin my future like you did in my past. I am leaving in a week." I was mumbling, trying to cover the passport with my clothes in the suitcase with one hand and carry my laptop like a baby with the other one. My hands were shaking. So was my voice.

I made my way back to the living room, where my father was talking to the agents.

"You are here for me," he said. "You got whatever you want. Let my daughter have her laptop."

"You are not in the position to tell me what to do," one agent said. He approached me, and I wrapped my arms tight around the laptop. "Give me the laptop. We'll give it back to you in two days, I swear," he said in a friendly tone.

I knew he was lying. They never give back the things they take. In 2001, when my father was in prison for his political activities, his magazine office was raided and its belongings confiscated. We haven't seen them since.

"I won't give it to you. I have private photos and videos. I don't want you to look at them," I cried.

"We're not interested in looking at them either," another agent replied, smirking and scratching his patchy beard.

"Don't you have a mother? Don't you have a sister? Don't you have a daughter? Do you like some strangers looking at their private photos?" I was trembling and struggling to shout as loud as I could. But the lump in my throat prevented me from shouting. The more I tried, the more I felt that I was choking.

Then suddenly, I could neither shout nor breathe. I sat on the sofa, pressing the laptop firmly against my chest, knowing that I'd rather die than leave it. My father panicked, trying to tell me something, but I couldn't hear him. I was gasping for air.

After what felt like an eternity, I heard my father's voice—"Have some water"—as he held out a glass.

I took a small sip and let the water slide down my throat. My father gently stroked my back.

"Be calm, darling," he said, "be calm." He gave me a pale smile. I saw how dry his lips were. Not just dry but parched. *What time is it?* I had no idea how much time had passed. My father hadn't broken his fast yet.

"You drink, Baba," I said, pushing the water glass toward him.

"I am okay," he said, setting the glass back on the table.

For the next half hour, the agents tried everything. Some came close to me and talked in a friendly manner. Some yelled and threatened. They played good cop, bad cop. I remained on the sofa, hugging my laptop as if it was the last thing left in my life.

This was no longer about that damn laptop. No, this was my one chance to resist tyranny face to face. For thirty years, I'd witnessed how they tortured, imprisoned, and restricted my father, over and over again, just because he could think differently. My revenge would be resistance, showing I did not fear their power.

"You are wasting our time," repeated the smirking agent. "Give the laptop and let us go."

"I am wasting time, or you are? You raid the house of innocent people as if you've found a terrorist," I said. "What did you find? Bombs? Guns? Look! Just books and papers." I pointed to the pile in the middle of the living room. "My father is a decent scholar," I cried, "not a terrorist!"

"Shut your mouth," a bad cop yelled. He was the oldest, barely in his thirties. I guessed he was the superior. He turned to my father. "If you don't take the laptop from your daughter, I'll use a taser. And I don't know what will happen next." He tucked his right hand against the small of his back under his loose khaki shirt. I was unsure what was there; perhaps the taser, or the gesture was meant to scare us.

I looked at my father. His face turned red as if all the blood in his body had rushed to his face. He stood up despite the pressure that two agents exerted on his shoulders.

"Do it. Go ahead," he yelled. "One thing you know very well is killing people. You want to kill her like Zahra Kazemi and Haleh Sahabi?" Pointing his finger at the bad cop, my father yelled, "Do it."

I had never seen my father like that. He bit his lower lip to stop the trembling.

I was an undergrad at the University of Tehran when Zahra Kazemi died in 2003. She was an Iranian-Canadian photojournalist, taking photos of families of political prisoners in front of the Evin prison in Tehran when she was arrested. A few days later, she died under torture, with Iranian authorities considering her death an accident. Her body was never returned to her family in Canada.

Eight years later, Ezat Sahabi, a prominent dissident and a friend of my father, passed away. Security officials broke up his funeral ceremony and struck his daughter, Haleh. My memories of that day are still fresh. Haleh was walking in the front row of the funeral procession, holding her father's photo to her chest, when suddenly she lay unconscious on the ground. The family was forced to bury her body in the darkness of that night, beside her father's.

When my father mentioned their names, my stomach sank. I was scared.

Will I die in front of Baba?

I closed my eyes and held my breath. I didn't want them to see the fear in my eyes. I said a prayer and slowly let my breath out. *I'm not going to give up,* I told myself.

Looking around the room, I saw distress on all the faces. The agents were under pressure from their boss. This was supposed to be one of their smooth, typically oppressive missions, but it was not going as planned. I could hear the phone calls, the whispering in each other's ears: "It's getting late. Haji wants us to wrap it up and get back to the base."

My father was terrified. They had threatened his daughter's life. I was frightened, too. I just wanted my father to come close and ask me to give up my laptop so everything would end.

But I knew he wouldn't do that. He knew I wasn't fighting for a machine. He knew all this was for something bigger, something deeper. I was fighting for my rights, for my freedom, for my dignity. He could not ask me to give up. He was the one who had taught me to stand up for all of these things and more.

There was no way of knowing what might happen next, but we could not step back. There was an invisible force, beyond our fear of our well-being, pushing us forward to resist. Perhaps it was the same force that had helped Nelson Mandela endure decades of unjust imprisonment, strengthened Rosa Parks as she fought segregation, and prevented Bobby Sands from stopping his hunger strike.

As a child of two dissidents, I grew up hearing stories of protests and resistance against injustice all around the world. When friends of my age were reading romance novels, I was reading about Mohammad Mosaddegh, Martin Luther King Jr., Mahatma Gandhi, Djamila Boupacha, and many other activists. I always wondered how people could risk their own life and safety for the sake of their beliefs. Until that moment in our living room, surrounded by those agents, I had never had a chance to take that risk myself.

Now, I knew that I might suffer, but I could not give up.

I have to resist, I told myself.

I opened my eyes. One of the agents attacked me, trying to grab the laptop, and then another agent came to help him. I bowed over the laptop on the sofa to protect it. From then on, the only sound I could hear was the echo of my voice in my head: *I won't give up, I won't give up, I won't give up*.

One agent pulled me so hard that I felt my hair tearing out of its roots. The scarf around my neck was progressively strangling me. I couldn't breathe. I had no choice but to lean back on the sofa. I looked at my father, a few steps away, was shouting and struggling towards me. Two agents grabbed his hands and shoved him up against the wall.

I wanted to tell him, "It's okay, Baba. It's not your fault." But the words would not come.

The agents were beating me so I would loosen my grip. The more they beat, the more I pressed my arms around the laptop. I felt a burning in my arms. Another agent positioned himself in front of me and grabbed the top of the laptop, pulling it toward himself. In a desperate reaction, I kicked him, causing him to fall back. This enraged the other agents. Within seconds, they all rushed toward me and began to beat me from all directions.

My hands grew numb. I couldn't resist anymore.

I heard a loud beeping sound in my ears, and everything became unmute again. I was on the floor. My clothes were ripped off, my glasses broken.

My laptop was in the hands of the smirking agent. He was laughing.

I wanted to puke.

"Get out of my house," my father yelled.

They packed everything like the spoils of war and left our home with triumphant gestures.

A few hours later, I stretched out my hand to turn on the faucet in the bathroom and noticed bruises on my wrist. I took off my clothes and checked my naked body in the mirror. I had other bruises and scratches on my arms, around my neck, and on my back. One agent had dug into my right arm so savagely that his nails had torn through my clothes and right into my skin, leaving marks.

I felt I had been raped.

I stepped into the shower, felt the warm water pouring over me, then turned the faucet to make the water hotter. I wanted it hot enough to burn my skin and wash away all the traces. I lathered my loofah with soap, tears sliding down my face. I could no longer hold them back.

I violently scrubbed my arms, trying to process what had

happened. With each scrub, I had a flashback. The pain in my heart made my legs numb. I sat down in the tub, wrapping my arms around my legs and hugging myself. I was shaking and crying uncontrollably.

What I had done to deserve such hatred and violence?

After a long time crying, I gathered my strength and climbed out of the tub. Drying off, I looked into the misty mirror. They were still there—all the bruises and the scratches. What had I expected, that I could wash them off?

I stomped on the bathroom floor as I stared into my eyes in the mirror. "I am going to leave you and never come back," I cried. "You never change. There will never be justice here."

I was talking to my motherland, blaming it for what had happened and for all the other injustices of the last thirty years I'd lived there. I yelled, "I hate you, I hate you, I hate you." And with each word, I stomped harder and harder.

That night in bed, I pulled the quilt over my head and curled up in the fetal position. I tried to sleep, but I saw the agents' faces laughing at me each time I closed my eyes. I stroked my injured arms and apologized to my body for how it had been treated. That night and for many nights after, sleep evaded me.

The raid changed all the plans for my last days in Iran. I canceled goodbye parties with my friends and family. I did not say goodbye to many people. I just wanted to leave. My father was worried that the security agents would report my resistance and prevent me from leaving the country. In his voice and eyes, I could see his desire for me to have freedom, to not be constrained as he had been.

*

"Flight TK083 for Montreal is boarding now," a voice announced.

I found myself in the line beside Aydin. I saw our reflection in the terminal window, each of us carrying a heavy backpack. I had buckled the waist and chest straps to keep my balance. Aydin had his instrument, a *tar*, slung over his right shoulder. He held the handle of his carry-on with his left hand. I was the same; my instrument, a *daf*, was in one hand and my carry-on in the other. The image of us in the window was unfamiliar to me. We looked weary, bulky, as if carrying our whole home with us.

I called my father. "Baba, we are departing." "Have a safe trip and enjoy your new home," he said.

The word "home" echoed strangely in my mind. *Where is my home? Am I leaving it behind or flying towards it?*

When the plane took off, I gazed out the window, capturing one last glimpse of my motherland. It shrank smaller and smaller beneath me. I didn't take my eyes off it until it vanished into the darkness.

I sensed a profound change within me, a feeling that I would never be the same person again and that land would never hold the same meaning. I knew I had lost my home at that moment, and the uncertainty of whether I would find a new one scared me.

THE BREAD

A few weeks after landing in Canada, I was passing by a Middle Eastern restaurant in downtown Ottawa. It was almost noon. A customer opened the door, and the aroma of freshly baked bread hit me. I took a deep breath. *I miss Iranian bread*, I thought.

That smell did something to me. It took me back to my childhood, to some deep level of memory I didn't know existed, and to Pari *khanoom*, Miss Pari, and her fresh bread in the mornings. I suddenly missed home. *Pari khanoom was right*, I thought, walking toward the bus station. *Fresh bread is the smell and taste of home.*

Bread is a staple in Iranian cuisine. I can eat bread for breakfast, lunch, and dinner and never grow tired. In any given neighborhood, there are bakeries that specialize in one kind of bread. In recent decades, these bakeries have been mechanized, but still, the *shater*, the baker, prepares the dough and bakes the bread in tandoor. Bread is baked three times a day—after sunrise, at noon, and before sunset—and at these times, there is always a line in front of the bakeries.

Modern bakeries carry baguettes, buns, and other Western-style breads, but these weren't common when I was growing up. Even sandwiches at home were made with flatbread, like lavash or *taftoon*. I could count on one hand the number of times I had a luxury-item baguette sandwich in my childhood.

When I was ten, my mother had two complex surgeries on one hand. The first was to remove a benign tumor from her right palm, and the second was to fix her ulnar nerve, which the surgeon had mistakenly cut during the first surgery. Between the surgeries and for months after, my mother was in constant pain. She couldn't sleep at nights. She would pace back and forth across the living room, her right arm folded on her chest, her left hand gripping the right elbow. She was moaning as if murmuring a sad lullaby for her hand to finally rest.

My energetic mother was suddenly in bed most of the time. She stopped all her activities outside the home and couldn't do much inside, either. Normally, she loved to take care of everything herself, but now she couldn't. My father was a full-time professor at the University of Tehran, working dawn to dusk, and my brother and I were in the sixth and the fourth grade, busy with school and homework. So, she hired Pari *khanoom* for help.

Pari *khanoom* was in her late thirties, small and chatty, with a limp. She had fallen from a tree when she was a child, and her broken leg was never set correctly. Pari *khanoom* would press the doorbell at 7 a.m. sharp each morning and wouldn't take her finger off the bell until someone opened the door. Thanks to her entering our lives, my brother and I needed no alarm to wake us up for school.

"Salaam, salaam, hello, hello, hello, everyone," she would yell as she came in, her voice rising more and more after each hello. The only thing that could compete with that voice were the clinking gold bangles she wore on her left wrist and their jingle-jangle sound, which never stopped.

She would start her work by preparing breakfast and washing the dishes from the night before, and all this time, she would talk nonstop about everything that had happened since she'd left the day before. There was the street cat, which had given birth to six kittens. There was Ali *agha*, Mr. Ali, the baker, who'd asked her to find a suitor for his daughter. There was the government, useless at taking care of the poor. Nothing escaped her attention. "A bright purple hue and gray are this year's colors," she once said. "I know it because everyone wears them."

My mother would sit at the kitchen table, drinking her milk tea and listening to her. Sometimes Pari *khanoom* would halt what she was doing and turn around to tell her story to my mother face to face. And if my mother left the room for any reason, Pari *khanoom* would yell, "Where are you? Come here. I want to tell you something."

All this changed my mother's gloomy mornings, stories that distracted mind and body from the painful, sleepless nights. Pari *khanoom* cheered my mother. I even saw her smiling once again.

"I know what's wrong with your hand," Pari *khanoom* pronounced one day. "It's an evil eye."

She then took an egg from the fridge and asked my mother to name anyone among family, friends, and even neighbors who might have evil eyes. "We should break this curse," she said.

I was eating breakfast at the kitchen table beside my mother, who was sipping her tea. I stopped chewing and looked straight at her. I didn't know where this line of questioning would end up, but it sounded exciting. Like Pari *khanoom*, I wanted my mother to name names.

She narrowed her eyes, looking doubtful, but settled into her seat and uttered the names one by one. Pari *khanoom* dutifully wrote them on the egg with a pencil till there was no white space on the shell.

"I think that's all," my mother said. Pari *khanoom* gave her an approving look and asked me to bring her two coins.

I dropped whatever I was eating and ran to my parents' room. When I returned to the kitchen, I found Pari *khanoom* cradling an empty bowl on the floor. I gave her the coins and plunked down next to her to watch. Pari *khanoom* held the egg between two coins with her left index finger and thumb over the bowl.

"Sima," she said loudly and pressed the coins. Nothing

happened. "Mrs. Gholami." Pari *khanoom* pressed the egg again. "Not this one," she said.

She circled the eggshell, saying the names out loud, one by one. Soon, the egg cracked on one name, but it did not break. She continued till the egg broke and plopped into the bowl.

"Look, it's her," Pari *khanoom* emphasized, smiling. "I didn't do that; the egg broke on its own."

My mother looked doubtful, but she didn't stop Pari *khanoom* or say a word. I guess deep down, she wanted to believe this was the reason for her pain, and now, with the evil eye vanquished, she would soon get better.

Pari *khanoom* then covered the egg-filled bowl with a lid and said, "I'll toss it into the river on my way back home. This is important, for the egg to flow away in running water."

After this momentous, curse-breaking event, we had burning *esfand* ceremonies every morning until my mother finally put a stop to them a week or so later. Pari *khanoom* would place the wild rue seeds on a special long-handled metal spoon and run it through a flame. Within seconds, the seeds would make popping sounds. When smoke rose from the burning seeds, she'd turn off the stove and circle the hot spoon over everyone's head while murmuring a prayer. I would close my eyes and bend my head, terrified that the hot seeds would fall and burn my hair. But when I opened my eyes, she was off, carrying the spoon all over our home. Smoke lingered in the air.

"It's good to ward off evil eyes," she'd say with satisfaction.

Pari *khanoom* brought back to us cleanliness, order, home-cooked meals, and comfort. But my favorite thing about that time with her was waking up to the intoxicating smell of bread. Every morning, she bought fresh bread on her way to our place. My mother never asked her to do so. It was Pari *khanoom*'s own sweet, kind gesture.

"Fresh bread is the taste and scent of home," she would say.

Before and after Pari *khanoom*, bread would be pulled out of the freezer and warmed up on the flame or toasted. My father would go to the bakery once a week to buy dozens of *taftoons*, the circular flat bread that is baked on the walls of a tandoor oven. My mother then would cut the *taftoons* into small pieces and pack them in the freezer. The only time we would eat warm, fresh bread was in the afternoons when my father came home with *taftoons*.

Pari *khanoom*'s fresh bread changed my relationship with mornings. Before then, I was never a fan of breakfast. I would eat everything by force, then leave for school. But the smell of bread stirred my appetite. I would slip into the kitchen every morning to find Pari *khanoom* opening her faded linen bread bag and pulling out the bread to let it breathe and cool on the kitchen table.

Every day she would buy a different kind, and I chose my breakfast accordingly. If *sangak*, rectangular, whole-wheat leavened flatbread, I ate cheese, walnuts, and sweet tea. Because *sangak* bakes in a dome-shaped tandoor with a pebbled surface, there would still be pebbles clinging to the bread when Pari *khanoom* pulled it from the bag.

"I asked the baker to make it special with poppy seeds," she would giggle as she tapped the pebbles off.

If she bought *taftoon*, I would eat butter and jam or butter and honey with milk. *Taftoon* is thin, which makes it ideal for runny toppings like honey. But with the long, oval-shaped *barbari* and its deliciously chewy, doughy ends, I would ask her to make an egg for me, sunny side up.

It took two years before my mother fully recovered, then she found a job for Pari *khanoom* in another home. I did not want her to go. I was used to her stories and her presence. On the last day, I hugged her. She pressed me to her petite body.

"Who is going to buy me fresh bread?" I asked.

She stroked my hair. "I will bring you fresh bread," she

said. “Every weekend.”

For ten years, she kept her promise. Then she fell ill and moved to another part of the city, too far from our home. But we have never lost contact. My mother still visits her from time to time. She also visits my parents’ home for New Year’s and other festive occasions.

Pari *khanoom* came to say goodbye the day before my flight to Canada. When I heard the doorbell sound, I told my mother, “It’s Pari *khanoom*.” We all knew how she rang the bell.

She came inside with two packs of fresh *sangak*s and *barbari*s.

“I bought them for you to take,” she said, scattering the bread on the table to breathe. “Keep them in the freezer. When you miss home, toast them and eat,” she said. “The smell and taste won’t be the same as fresh ones, but it is better than nothing.”

I looked at her as she spoke. After twenty years, she was unchanged, only with more wrinkles and no bangles with their jingle-jangle sound. I jumped off my chair, hugged her tight, and thanked her for the bread. She giggled and hugged me back.

*

“I’m going to bake bread,” I told Aydin after the smell of fresh bread that wafted from the Middle Eastern restaurant stirred memories I needed to retrace.

Aydin gave me a suspicious look. “Okay,” he said. He did not know how serious I was.

I searched for recipes and studied YouTube videos, and after a couple of hours, I was convinced that *barbari* was the easiest Iranian bread I could bake at home.

Each day in the kitchen was an experiment, and my attempts were failures, but once I made some adjustments, good-looking, delicious bread came out of the oven. It was not *barbari,* though. Not even close. Aydin encouraged me to try more and even came to help.

After two months of baking almost every day, I decided to stop. The breads I baked were excellent, much better than those I bought from local bakeries. Yet, I did not want to replace the taste and scent that filled my memories with these so-called New World *barbaris*.

Canada is my new home; I'll eat its food, I told myself. I changed my breakfast routine and started eating different varieties of fruit yogurts and cereals. I began regularly eating hot dogs, burgers, and pizza and also introduced myself to frozen food I could pop in the microwave. Five minutes, and voilà! There was my lasagna, my chicken teriyaki, and my fries. I bought every kind of frozen food, hoping each time they would turn out like the picture on the package. They never did.

One fall day, I was shopping at the supermarket when I saw everyone had a turkey in their cart. *Should I buy one, too, and try my first Thanksgiving with a turkey?* I had never cooked a turkey. I eyed the frozen turkeys and chose one of the biggest.

That afternoon, I was checking recipes for how to cook a turkey when Aydin came home with two turkeys in his hands.

"They were on sale," he said. "I thought it is a good deal to eat turkey instead of chicken for a while."

"Sure, it is," I said cautiously. Now we had three turkeys. We just needed to figure out where to store them. We lived in an apartment with a compact refrigerator and its small freezer.

"We can cook them all and pack them in smaller portions to put in the freezer," Aydin said.

On Thanksgiving Day, it was just the two of us. A big turkey lay in the middle of the table, decorated with loads of vegetables. Two smaller ones were in the oven, still cooking.

"It's huge," Aydin said. I nodded. The bird looked amazing

with its golden, crispy skin.

"It's going to take days to finish it," I said, looking at Aydin struggling to carve the turkey.

That turkey would be good for twenty people, but since we were new in town and we had no friends, it took a week or two for us to finish. By then, I was out of ideas for how to make a new dish from leftover turkey. I'd made everything—soups, salads, casserole, chili, sandwiches, pasta, stews, and cutlets.

We were thrilled when we had our last meal of Thanksgiving leftovers—only, we still had twenty packs of cooked turkey in the freezer and no space to store anything else. Every meal, including Iranian stews, was made with turkey for months.

"Two more," Aydin enthused one day as he checked the freezer.

For two years after, I couldn't tolerate the taste or smell of turkey. For Thanksgiving, I cooked rice with *ghormeh sabzi*, an Iranian stew made with herbs, red kidney beans, and lamb. I did not even think about turkey.

*

When I immigrated, I stepped into a land with no memories, severing my connection to the familiar. I thought detaching from memories of my motherland would help me forget what I had lost.

I was mistaken.

Over the past decade of living in Canada as an immigrant, I have realized the importance of cherishing aspects of those memories that I can still trace. I now understand why immigrants throughout history have recreated spaces, foods, rituals, and other elements from their past homes in their new ones. These recreations may not be identical replicas, but they carry strong elements that evoke a sense of what has been left behind. It's not just about flavor, smell, sound, or the act itself; it's about remembering, which gives a sense of continuity, belonging, reliving, revisiting, and, more than anything, identity.

These remembrance rituals help us cope with loss and shorten the distance between the past and the present. Much like Pari *khanoom*'s joyful stories of the outside world that helped my mother—isolated in her room—cope with her loss of health and social life.

Today, I sometimes bake *barbari* and sometimes buy *sangak* from Iranian bakeries in Toronto. I enjoy eating them even though they don't taste like the ones Pari *khanoom* used to buy. Whether I pair *barbari* with sunny side up eggs or *sangak* with cheese and walnuts for breakfast, the familiar rituals, despite the different tastes, provide a strong sense of home.

We cook a turkey on occasion for Thanksgiving and invite some friends. Sometimes we cook *ghormeh sabzi*. The food at our home is not totally Iranian any more than it is totally Canadian.

THE LUT DESERT*

I still feel my heart race faster whenever I recall those winter evenings in Montreal, trudging through deep snow, bundled up in ten kilos of winter clothes and boots. It felt as if I were moving in slow motion, taking one step, pausing to inhale and exhale, and then repeating the process all over again.

Every now and then, I would lower the wool scarf tightly wrapped around my face, allowing the fog on my eyeglasses to disperse. I would pause briefly, inhaling the air at minus twenty or thirty degrees Celsius, feeling my entire respiratory system freeze as the air found its way to my lungs. Then I would readjust the scarf around my face, instantly causing my glasses to fog up once again. I would rather walk with hazy vision over the risk of my nose becoming exposed to the bitter cold.

In the very first session of our integration classes in Canada, the instructor dropped a bombshell on us: "If you don't cover your ears and nose, they might freeze and even fall off." As a newcomer, it was far from the warm, welcoming news I had expected. To make matters even more unsettling, she went on to say, "In this situation, put the fallen part in your mouth and rush to the emergency room."

Sitting among fellow immigrants from the Middle East, North Africa, and South America, we were all taken aback. Not a single sound escaped our lips. It felt as if we were watching a scene from a zombie movie.

I never bothered to check if what our instructor said was

* An excerpt of this story was published in *The New Quarterly*, May 2020.

true, but I believed her when I experienced my first winter in Montreal. By then, Aydin and I had been in Canada for six months, still struggling to find jobs. Our savings were running low, so we spent as little as possible.

We began purchasing groceries from a nearby Chinese store because of its slightly lower prices compared to other places. Every week, we made a routine visit to the store, consistently selecting the same items. Our protein choice was chicken, accompanied by vegetables like tomatoes, cucumbers, and carrots. For fruits, we opted for oranges and apples. As for our indulgence, we would buy a banana cake, which paired perfectly with vanilla ice cream.

We had to cancel our mobile phone and home Internet services. Every day, we would pack our food in the morning and go to the University of Montreal, where Aydin was taking some courses at the time. Aydin would attend his classes while I found a spot in the cafeteria, using the available Internet to search and apply for jobs. We would spend the entire day on campus before returning home in the evening.

The distance from our apartment building to the university was about two kilometers, roughly three bus stops away. However, we never took the bus, to save on the fare. Walking or biking would have been pleasant during the summer, but not during the harsh winter months.

One evening in the middle of February, we trudged down Woodbury Avenue, returning home. The snow was deep, reaching up to our knees, and the street appeared deserted, as if no human being lived there. The cars parked along the sides of the street were covered in snow, resembling frosted cakes. The temperature felt nearly minus forty degrees Celsius. Aydin walked ahead, leading the way and shielding me from the relentless wind.

With my head down, I focused on each step, carefully following in Aydin's footsteps. Suddenly, I felt a tightness in my chest.

I lifted my head, and through my foggy glasses, I saw Aydin's figure just a few steps ahead, blanketed in the falling snow.

"Aydin," I called out.

He turned around to check on me. "Are you okay?" he asked. His eyebrows and eyelashes were white and frozen, resembling a giant snowman. It was a sight that would usually make me laugh, but not at that moment.

I tugged my scarf down, desperately gasping for air. I immediately regretted it as the wind whipped snow into my face. "I can't breathe anymore," I said.

"Just a few more minutes, honey. We'll be home soon." I knew that under normal weather conditions, it would only take us twenty minutes to walk home from here. However, in this condition, it would take much longer.

I didn't say anything.

Aydin took a few steps backward. He outstretched his hand, grasped mine tightly, and pulled me closer to him. In silence, we made our way hand in hand toward home. The freezing air made it hard to breathe, let alone to talk. Aydin would squeeze my hand, silently assuring me, *I'm here. Everything will be okay.*

I didn't have the strength to return the gesture by pressing his back. With every crunch of snow beneath my winter boots, I whispered to myself, *Just one more step.*

Later on, I read in the news that February 2015 was Montreal's coldest February in over a century. Despite visiting the city a couple of times during the summer after we moved away, and enjoying those trips, my connection with Montreal never fully recovered. The memories of that harsh winter have left an enduring impression, casting Montreal in my mind as an inhospitable frozen tundra.

We moved to Burlington, Ontario, in the spring, as Aydin found a job there. People assured us that winters in Burlington would be nothing like Montreal, and they were right.

However, after surviving our first winter in Canada, Aydin and I were sure we needed a car to tackle the next one.

"No more trudging through deep snow," I firmly declared to Aydin, who agreed.

During that spring and summer, we managed to save some money. When fall arrived, Aydin searched for a second-hand car that would fit our modest budget. After diligent searching, he came across a great deal, but the car was in Laval, six hundred kilometers from our Burlington home. Despite the additional bus fare and paperwork costs, Aydin concluded that the trip was worthwhile.

Aydin took an overnight bus from Toronto to Laval and bought the car in the morning. He quickly finished all the paperwork and drove back home in a blue Hyundai Elantra all within twenty-four hours.

The following day, as he was giving me a ride to work, we made an unexpected discovery: the car had no air conditioning.

"What? It can't be!" Aydin shouted in disbelief.

He stopped a car in a parking lot, anxiously searching for the air-conditioner all over the car. I couldn't help myself. I started laughing.

"Why are you laughing? It's not funny," Aydin said.

"Sorry, honey. It reminds me of my father's car," I said, trying to compose myself.

"I checked everything except the air conditioning. I never even thought about it," he murmured, searching for any trace of an air-conditioner, hoping to find it hidden somewhere.

"It's all right. At least we have a heater, which is all we need during winter," I said. "We can manage without air conditioning in the summer. We're not in a desert here," I added, trying to comfort him.

*

I grew up in the eighties and nineties in Iran. My parents'

travel methods were basically focused on road trips because they wanted my brother and me to see and feel our diverse country and culture in a tangible way. So, instead of flying to our destination, we drove there. "The trip is not just about the destination. It's about the journey," my father would always say, and he truly believed in that.

We would swivel around in our seats and watch landscapes transform through car windows. We would stop on the way and visit historic sites. We socialized with local people with different dialects or languages, outfits, and customs. We would taste regional food, sweets, and savories we weren't used to eating at home.

My parents would make spontaneous stops whenever they found something interesting, like when they spotted local farmers selling their produce by the roadside. Once, while returning from a trip to Kermanshah, my mother noticed some villagers selling *zo*, a local vegetable that she had heard had medicinal benefits. She decided to buy the vegetable, not just for tasting, but in a large quantity to bring back home.

The next day, my mother cooked the vegetable as directed by the locals, using two big pots in our kitchen. As it simmered, the smell of rotten eggs began to fill the house. The longer it cooked, the more the odor intensified, quickly becoming overwhelming. My brother and I, desperate for fresh air, flung open all the windows and stuck our heads out, trying to escape the suffocating stench. The scent was so intense that our neighbors in the building complex began knocking on our door, one after the other, concerned that we might have a gas leak.

Despite the chaos, my mother remained unfazed, reminding us of the vegetable's many health benefits and insisting we should try the local food.

My parents' adventures during our trips would not end with visiting historic monuments or tasting local foods. If a sign directed us to a factory, my father would take the detour without hesitation. He would enter the factory and request a tour. Surprisingly, we were always welcomed. I guess it was also interesting for the managers of these factories to see a typical family show up in the middle of nowhere, asking for a visit. It was not a normal request. Not only would they give us a tour of the factory, but they would also offer us their guest residence to rest and eat before we headed back on the road. On our trips, we toured a tannery, a sugarcane mill, a still company, and even a salt mine—to name a few.

Once, on our way to Sanandaj, my father saw a sign for Mahabad City and remembered that he'd had a colleague from there when he was a chemistry teacher in Qasr-e Shirin, a small city near the western border of Iran, shortly after completing his bachelor's degree, almost twenty-five years ago.

"Let's find him," he announced with excitement.

Mahabad was a small city back then, and people generally knew each other in such close-knit communities, especially if someone had a unique skill like teaching English. My father stopped the car and approached a group of young adults sitting on the sidewalk in front of their stores. He asked them if they knew Mr. Enayati.

"I know an English teacher named Enayati," one of them said, standing up. When my father explained that he was a friend looking for him, the man agreed to take us to his house.

My father rang the bell, and there he was—Mr. Enayati, staring at my father after twenty-five years. At first, Mr. Enayati didn't recognize him, but when my father started speaking, he jumped up and hugged him.

"I know this voice," he said.

We did not have a plan to stop at Mahabad, but Mr. Enayati and his family warmly hosted us at their house for a week as if we had been friends for years.

Another time, on our trip to Lake Urmia, one of the largest saline lakes in the world, my father decided to collect some mud from its shore to bring to Tehran.

"This is good for joint-swelling," he said while digging into the black, thick mud. He asked my brother and me to join him.

We hesitantly rolled up our pants legs and stepped in. I dipped into the mud, covering my leg up to the knees. The cool mud squished between my toes as I tried to keep my balance in the slippery earth beneath my feet.

"It smells like sewage," I said, covering my nose with my scarf.

"It's the smell of the minerals in the mud. Don't take this resource for granted. People spend so much money on mud therapy in the West," my father said while filling a barrel with the mud.

The smell from the mud barrel in the trunk accompanied us for the rest of the trip, and even after removing the barrel, it lingered for weeks.

To complete his mud therapy thesis, my father gave the barrel to Mrs. Khaleghi, his friend's mother who suffered from arthritis, and instructed her to soak her legs in the mud for an hour daily. The poor woman diligently followed this routine for two months, patiently awaiting results. Eventually, the family couldn't bear the smell of mud throughout their house any longer, so they disposed of it.

One of our regular road trips took place in the summer. We would drive from Tehran, where we lived, to Birjand, my father's hometown in the eastern part of Iran, near the Afghanistan border. This was a distance of more than 1,200 kilometers.

The trip would take us twelve hours, and for most of it, we would drive through the Lut Desert. For one five-hour stretch, there were almost no signs of civilization—no gas stations, restaurants, tea houses, nothing. It was just me, my parents, my brother, and the desert. If we were lucky, we might see a car or a truck pass us every one or two hours.

Back then, this area was remote. It was so remote that the

United States chose to secretly land helicopters there in their failed 1980 operation to rescue US embassy hostages. We learned about this failed operation in school and how the sandstorm caused difficulties for the Americans and made them turn back. However, I was usually the only student in my class who had seen the area, which made me feel important.

There were other routes my father could have taken that didn't go directly through the desert, but he preferred this one. "It is a shortcut and will save us hours," he would say. But now I think the main reason was that he liked the emptiness of the desert and wanted to escape from the hustle and bustle of the cities. I liked it too.

Back then, there was no mobile phone or iPad to watch movies or play games. I couldn't read a book as I was prone to motion sickness. But I was never bored of watching the desert. It was as if the desert hypnotized me with its silence. There was just the sound of the road beneath the tires.

We drove at a fairly high speed, but it seemed we weren't moving. Every stretch we passed looked like the one before it. No matter which direction I looked, all I could see was sand. The wind would blow the sand into the air, where it would briefly dance and then fall. This cycle would be repeated again and again. The road shimmered ahead of us, almost like water on the surface. And, in some parts, a light blanket of sand covered the road, hiding it from view.

My brother and I sometimes would sit cross-legged on our seats, facing backward, leaning on the back of the front seats. The car's rear window functioned like a TV screen for us. "Look! It's like a snowman," my brother would say as he pointed to a fluffy cloud in the enormous blue sky above us. And I tried to follow his finger's direction. We would play this game for hours, and most of the time, ended in a fight.

My father's whole family lived in Birjand. My brother and I were excited about this annual trip because we enjoyed visiting our aunt and uncle and playing with our cousins for a full month. But there was a big issue with these road trips: our car.

My father owned a Paykan, the first Iranian-made car. The design of the Paykan looked like a Hillman Hunter vehicle produced in the UK in the sixties and seventies. But all of the Paykan's parts were made and installed locally.

My father was all about supporting nationally made products. For as long as I can remember, foreign brands of tea and rice were forbidden in our home. He believed we should support our local farmers and producers to help the country's economy. And this extended to our car.

The Paykan didn't have air conditioning. Imagine driving in the Lut Desert, the hottest place on earth, where, in the middle of the day, temperatures reach higher than forty-five degrees Celcius, without air conditioning.

My brother, Mohammad, and I would roll down all the windows, letting the air blow through every opening in the car, but we'd just get pelted by the hot air pouring in. Everything would get sticky in the car with the heat. My neck felt slick with sweat as did my forehead. My hair stuck to my scalp, and my thighs would make sounds when I tried to peel them from the seat.

My mother would try everything that she could think of to keep us cool. She would hang a wet cloth on her open window so we would feel a cool breeze in the back seat when the wind blew through the cloth. But before long, the cloth would get warm, so she became more creative after a few of these road trips.

A few nights before our trip, she would fill empty yogurt containers with water and freeze them. She kept these ice packs in a blue Coleman cooler underneath her feet, and during the road trip, she would wrap the ice packs in a plastic bag and a thin towel and hand them to us to put on our heads and bodies.

I stuck the ice pack to my cheeks and neck, then on top of my head, then rolled up my shirt and put it on my belly. I would repeat the cycle a couple of times till the pack melted.

Thanks to our ancestors, there were still abandoned *āb-anbārs*, cisterns, on the roadside. They were our getaways before we lost our minds in the heat. The cistern is a reservoir for drinking water that was historically built on caravan routes in Iran. A vaulted passageway leads down to a reservoir under the ground, which is cool and pleasant.

"Baba, *āb-anbār*, *āb-anbār*," Mohammad and I would yell when we saw its dome roof and two chimney-like structures, wind catchers, on both sides.

My father would pull over, and we'd run inside the cistern and down the stairs. After the first few steps down, there was no trace of hot weather. We played around while my parents drank tea or lay in the shadow of the cistern's wind catchers. Then, we resumed the trip once again.

We would complain a lot about the car and ask my father to buy one with air conditioning. It was our constant discussion at home. But he would always say, "No, we need to support our national products." He didn't buy another car until the production of the Paykan was discontinued in the early twenty-first century.

By the time he finally bought a car with air conditioning, my brother and I had grown up and had our own ways of traveling.

In 2014, a decade after my last trip to Birjand, I found myself in the Lut Desert on the road toward my father's hometown with Aydin. Canada had just granted us our immigration visa, and we were preparing to fly there in a few months. I suggested to Aydin that we go to Birjand to say goodbye to my family, but more than that, I wanted to show him my roots. Perhaps I also wanted to remind myself.

"Can you turn off the air conditioning?" I asked Aydin in the middle of the Lut Desert. He gave me a weird look, but he turned it off.

I rolled down the car window and closed my eyes. I heard the tires on the road. I felt the heat slap my face. I smelled the sand and tasted the salt.

I saw my father tying a damp cloth around his neck and drying the sweat dripping off his face.

My mother stretching her sunburned hands towards me in the back seat to fan me.

My brother sleeping peacefully beside me, a cap protecting his face from the harsh rays of the desert sun.

"What is it?" Aydin asked.

"Nothing," I said.

No words could express what I was feeling and what I was remembering.

*

Thanks to that blue Hyundai Elantra, we didn't have a repeat of our first winter experience in Canada. However, Aydin sold the car before summer and bought another one. The first thing he checked on the new car was the air conditioning.

Once, in the middle of that summer, we were on the road somewhere between Burlington and Toronto. The radio was on, and there was a discussion about global warming.

"This summer is notable for having some of the most enduring heat on record. Going by the average temperature from May until now, 2016 was Toronto's hottest summer ever," one of the guests said.

"At least we were prepared this time," Aydin said, and we laughed.

THE WHITE MULBERRY

In June 2015, almost a year after I landed in Canada, my father was arrested and imprisoned at Evin Prison.

Since the raid of the intelligence agents on our house, my father had been under pressure from the hardliners to stop his peaceful political activities. However, he never gave up. Through his writings and speeches, my father continued to encourage the government to solve the nuclear problem with the world and to restate his position that a sustainable future for Iran could only be achieved through the release of political prisoners, free and fair elections, and an improvement in the human rights situation. Consequently, a year after the raid, when the threats had not worked on him, he was imprisoned in order to be finally silenced.

The morning that news of my father's arrest reached me, I found myself sitting on a bench overlooking Lake Ontario in downtown Burlington. I gazed at the water for hours while reflecting on the same questions: *What should I do? Should I continue my life as is, as a new immigrant trying to adapt to my new country, or should I start advocating for my father?*

I was still struggling to find myself in Canada. Immigration for me was not just a physical journey from one land to another; it was like I was reborn as an adult in a new world. Suddenly, no one was there to guide me on how to talk, behave, or what to do when encountering unfamiliar situations. From finding a family doctor to renting a house, I was expected to figure out everything on my own. These simple ordeals would drain all my energy, leaving me questioning whether I should further complicate my already challenging life.

I knew advocating for a political prisoner would be a full-time physical and emotional commitment. I had witnessed how my mother sacrificed her social life to advocate for my father when he was imprisoned for the first time in 2001, and I wondered if I wanted to make the same sacrifice.

The joyful sounds of a group of kids from the beach distracted me from the nonstop questions in my mind. They were chasing one another around and shooting water pistols. The scene encouraged me to walk towards the beach. I removed my shoes and dipped my bare feet in the warm sand. A few steps in, and I felt relaxed. Earthing was what I needed.

After a long walk on the beach, I found refuge in the shadow of a tree. As I adjusted my position on the sand, I felt something round and sticky underneath my hand. *A white mulberry!* I was surprised.

I looked up and realized I was sitting under the shadow of a mulberry tree. Without hesitation, I jumped up and started picking the ripe mulberries, one by one, within reach. As the oval-shaped, sweet berries melted in my mouth, old, good memories revived.

*

White mulberry picking was an annual ceremony in our family during my childhood. Once a year in late spring or early summer, we would visit Mr. Lotfi, my father's friend who owned a big white mulberry tree in his front yard. Parham, Mr. Lotfi's son, would climb the tree and gently shake its branches one by one while we held a white sheet below to catch the falling fruit. Within moments, tons of mulberries would rain down from the tree.

We were careful not to pile up too many mulberries on the sheet, as the pressure of the top ones would mash down the bottom ones. So, there would be several rounds of picking.

After each round, we would transfer the berries into flat baskets and sit in the yard, eating until we could not eat anymore. Mrs. Lotfi would bring us *dough*, a yogurt-water-salt drink cooled with ice cubes.

"Drink. It will prevent stomach-upset from eating too many mulberries," she would say.

My father would always be the most excited about mulberry picking, likely due to his childhood experiences. He grew up in a village where the white mulberry tree was treated as sacred. They believed that if they broke the branches or cut the trunk, a spell of misfortune would be cast on their lives. The main reason was that it served as one of the main food sources for the villagers during its picking seasons.

"People, especially the poor, would eat mulberries for breakfast and dinner, which would be enough to sustain them," my father would say.

A common practice in the village was to plant a mulberry tree in a public area and donate its fruits to the community so that those who did not own a tree could access food. The nature of the mulberry tree made it perfect for their goal because the fruits don't ripen at the same time, allowing villagers to enjoy fresh berries every day for two months. They would also sun-dry the extra mulberries and use them as snacks during winter, mixing them with other locally available nuts like walnuts and almonds.

Later on, a few villagers, such as my uncle's wife, *Bibi*, benefited from the leaves of the mulberry trees to raise silkworms and produce silk. Initially, they used the silk for their own needs, sewing handkerchiefs or tablecloths, but later they began selling it and making a good profit.

During one of our visits to my uncle in the village, when I was around ten, my father gathered all of us, including the first and second cousins, and announced that we would learn about silk production that afternoon. He then led us to the back room of the house, which had been off-limits to us that summer.

*

My uncle owned a large bungalow-style house with a big courtyard. The stable was on the left side of the courtyard, where he kept a couple of goats and a cow. There were also a bunch of hens and a roaster that freely roamed around the courtyard. Every morning, *Bibi* or one of my cousins would milk the cow and collect the eggs for breakfast.

A couple of *qanāts* were the only source of water in the village. *Qanāt* is an ancient water transportation system consisting of a series of well-like shafts connected by gently sloping tunnels that bring underground water to the surface. The *mazhar* of one of the *qanāts*, where the water flows above ground, was right in front of my uncle's house. A daily chore at his house was to collect water from the *mazhar* and fill the water barrels inside the house. One barrel was inside the toilet at the corner of the courtyard, and the larger barrel stood in the courtyard on a cement platform and served as a sink for washing hands and dishes.

My favorite part of staying at my uncle's house was collecting water from the *mazhar* and washing the dishes after each meal. I would squat or sit on a short-legged stool, and as I rinsed each dish under the barrel tap, my imagination would transport me to the worlds of my favorite cartoons. I dreamed of living in the same eras as *Katri, Girl of the Meadows*, *Les Misérables*, and *The Story of Perrine.*

The courtyard led to the house through a blue wooden door that opened into a long, wide corridor paved with smooth, glossy cement. This corridor was a practical space for daily chores and farm-related activities, such as cleaning *zereshk*, berberis, my uncle's main crop. Women workers would sit along the corridor, circling around piles of fresh berberis branches in the center. A tunnel of golden hues streamed through each opening in the high ceiling, casting large, radiant circles on the red berries. Dust particles swirled in the shimmering beams, mingling with the tangy scent of *zereshk* and the lively chatter of the workers—a scene that no camera could capture and no words could describe.

The corridor ended with a turn to the right, leading to the largest room at the back of the house, which my uncle occasionally used for hosting big parties. It was my favorite room, always cooler and more inviting than the others. The floor was covered with large, fine carpets, and narrow mattresses lined the rectangular space. Colorful, handmade cushions embroidered with flowers and birds were propped against the walls, allowing people to sit on the mattresses and lean comfortably on the cushions. My brother and I along with our cousins would sneak into the room to play, but that summer it was locked. And we were all curious to see what was hiding behind those closed doors.

My father led us into the room, and I found it completely transformed from how I remembered it. The room was now filled with shelves covered in mulberry leaves, with silkworms resting on them. Some were eating the leaves, creating a polka-dot effect, while others had woven egg-shaped cocoons around themselves. My father switched to his chemistry-professor mode and gave a scientific explanation about how the chemical reactions transform the cellulose in the leaves into silk, a topic that I doubt many, myself included, understood.

In conclusion of his speech, my father always drew a moral for the audience, whether as a father, professor, or political activist. On that day, he concluded by encouraging us to observe nature more carefully and learn from it. "Like Alexis Carrel, a Nobel laureate," he said.

"He spent months studying silk production and applied the techniques to suture veins," my father explained. He paused for a second to ensure we understood the significance of his work. "It was a revolution in surgery, as it made organ transplantation between individuals possible."

*

"Are these edible?" A passerby woman's voice brought me back from my uncle's house to the present moment in Burlington Beach.

"White mulberries," I answered. "Do you want some?" I stretched my hand and offered her a handful of ripe berries I had picked.

She hesitantly took one and popped it into her mouth. "Too sweet!" she exclaimed. Her green eyes sparkled, and the freckles scattered across her upper cheeks and the bridge of her nose seemed to glow with excitement, like a small child discovering hidden chocolates in the cupboard.

She then joined me in picking and eating white mulberries. I shared my childhood memories of mulberry-picking and my uncle's silk production while she recounted stories of her grandfather's farm. We both enjoyed the conversation, discovering how our lives on different continents had many similarities.

"Why did you come to Canada?" she asked.

"There were too many reasons," I replied. "But the most important one was that I wanted to be free." To ensure she understood, I explained that Iran had no freedom of thought or expression.

"I hope you feel free here," she said.

Do I feel free? I asked myself.

I smiled at her without saying anything, but I found the answer to the question that I'd been pondering all day.

I had left behind everything I held dear in pursuit of freedom in this new land: my loved ones, with whom I'd cried and laughed, traveled and shared meals, who had held my hands and embraced me when I needed it most; the places that had given me comfort, where I'd found refuge and created lasting memories; and the rituals that had made life feel familiar and safe. But in that moment, I realized that freedom wasn't tied to a physical place —it was a state of being, one I could never attain as long as my father remained imprisoned.

I decided to fight for the freedom stolen from me, not only in my motherland but also here, miles away in Canada. This fight had begun the day our house was raided in Tehran, and it was time to revive it. I knew that if I did this, I would never be able to return to Iran. Words cannot express the wrenching pain I felt and still feel by thinking about that, but I couldn't back down from my decision.

The next day, I quit my volunteering job at the museum and threw myself into planning. Unsure of where to begin, I started reaching out to scientific organizations. Many of these had supported my father during his imprisonment in 2001, and I hoped they would do it again.

Organizations like the American Chemical Society, the National Academy of Sciences, Scholars at Risk, and the Committee of Concerned Scientists all responded with unwavering support. They sent appeal letters to Iranian authorities demanding my father's release and stood by me until this happened.

But I didn't stop there. I took my advocacy to a broader audience. I wrote open letters to Iranian authorities, gave interviews to the media, published articles in journals, and launched a Facebook page to share my father's story and raise awareness about his situation. I met with Dr. Shaheed in Toronto, the UN special rapporteur on the human rights situation in Iran at the time. I also connected with other officials and human rights advocates in other parts of the world, demanding they use their power to release my father.

In December, six months into my father's detention, I had an idea to intensify the pressure on Iranian authorities. I decided to launch a petition addressed to the Iranian president, urging my father's release and seeking endorsements from scholars worldwide.

I shared my plan with Mohammad and Aydin, but they were both skeptical of the idea.

"How do you get their signatures?" Aydin asked.

"I'll reach out to them via email," I said.

"If you obtain fifteen to twenty signatures, that would be good," Mohammad suggested.

This conversation wasn't encouraging, but I was determined to put my plan in motion. I had been advocating for my father for half a year, but despite all my efforts, there was no sign of any change in his situation. I realized it was time to amplify this advocacy by bringing more voices to the cause.

I gathered the faculty email addresses of top-ranked universities in the US, Canada, and Europe. I sent individual emails to each recipient and told my father's story. I attached the open letter and asked whether they would endorse it.

Around 5:00 p.m. on the first day, I discovered I couldn't send any more emails. A message from Google informed me that my Gmail account had been suspended for twenty-four hours. A quick search revealed that sending over three hundred emails in a single day had triggered the suspension. I created a new Gmail account and resumed sending emails. When that account was also suspended, I moved on to create a third one and continued my efforts.

By the second day's end, emails filled my inbox. Professors from prestigious institutions such as Harvard, MIT, and Yale, alongside Nobel laureates in physics and chemistry, had not only read my email but also expressed their solidarity by signing the letter.

Two weeks later, I sent the petition to the Iranian president with 370 signatures. It exploded like a bombshell, both inside and outside Iran. Prestigious journals such as *Nature* and *Science* covered the news of the petition, and unexpectedly, some newspapers in Iran reported on the journal's reactions.

A few days after sending the letter, my mother visited

the prosecutor's office to follow up on my father's long-delayed request for a doctor's visit. The prosecutor, enraged by my advocacy efforts, replied, "Tell your daughter to stop her activities, or you will never see your husband free again." My mother stood firm and assured him that, having raised me, she knew I would never stop fighting for justice.

This was the first time the authorities reacted to my advocacy efforts. For the past months, they had not replied to any letters and had remained silent about the petitions. I had assumed they were ignoring everything, but hearing that my activities had frustrated them, I felt an overwhelming sense of pride for the first time in six months of advocating for my father. I had kept the promise I made to myself that day under the mulberry tree: "I will be a thorn in their sides. They will have no choice but to release Baba to get rid of me," I had vowed, with the tree standing as my silent witness.

*

In the summer of 2017, two years after my first visit, I returned to the mulberry tree. This time, Aydin and a few Iranian friends joined me. We picked white mulberries and enjoyed a picnic by the beach.

"I didn't think there were white mulberries in Canada. How did you find this tree?" one of our friends asked.

I paused, searching for the right words. "I just happened to pass by it," I replied with a small smile.

I kept my encounter with the tree a secret. I wasn't ready to share what I had experienced beneath its branches that day and the months that followed. I still needed time to process the marathon of advocacy I had endured.

While Aydin and the others headed to the water, I stayed behind, lying in the tree's shade. I gazed up at its branches, adorned with clusters of white berries that glimmered like gold in the sunlight.

THE LAST LEAF

My father's arrest cast a dark shadow over our family plans during the summer of 2015. Mohammad would get married in August and defend his PhD thesis in September. We were supposed to spend that summer in Amsterdam, where he lived, and celebrate these two significant events. We did, but without my father.

I flew to Amsterdam from Canada and joined my mother, who had arrived a few days earlier from Iran. We settled into a condo Mohammad had rented for us. It was joyful to reunite with my mother and brother after a year and to be together shortly after my father's arrest. However, before long, Mohammad and I became busy with our activities.

Mohammad was occupied with his wedding preparations and his thesis. I was also immersed in my advocacy activities. Most of the time, I was in front of my laptop, sending emails or talking to people. We unintentionally abandoned our mother, who had come to Amsterdam to fill her loneliness with her children. But, as always, she found a way to bring light to the darkness.

One quiet afternoon, as I poured tea in the kitchen, I overheard my mother's voice drifting from the backyard. I tiptoed toward the kitchen door and caught a glimpse of her chatting with the woman next door, who was about the same age as her. The backyards in that condo had no barriers, enabling an unobstructed view between the two women. They were seated in the shadow cast by the building in the backyard, sipping tea. My mother offered the woman some *sohan*, traditional Persian saffron brittle toffee, and, with a caring gesture, pointed at her teeth, trying to warn her.

"It's hard," she said in English.

The woman nodded as if she understood the message and cautiously took a bite of the *sohan*. She then said, "Mmmm," conveying that she enjoyed it.

Apart from Farsi, my mother can communicate in simple English, while the woman next door only spoke Dutch and Spanish. Throughout that summer, the two women would sit in their respective backyards, exchanging tea, snacks, and food, conversing in languages neither understood.

I once discovered my mother teaching her how to wrap grape leaves to make dolma using only gestures. She grabbed a spoonful of the filling and then looked at our neighbor; when she nodded, my mother placed it in the middle of the grape leaf. My mother looked at her again for confirmation and slowly wrapped the leaf while ensuring she followed. They sat at our kitchen table for an hour, wrapping all the dolma without exchanging words.

On another day, my mother treated us to delicious tacos.

"We made them with Maria," she said.

"Who is Maria?" Mohammad asked.

"Our neighbor," she replied. "She is Mexican, married to a Turkish man. I taught her how to make dolma," she said.

"I bet her husband is so happy about that," Mohammad said, and we all laughed.

Sometimes, they would call me and Maria's son, as we could speak English together, to act as translators, helping them understand each other's messages. Once, Maria wanted to tell my mother to get a mobility scooter like the one she had. She asked her son to tell me the government would pay for it. Apparently, my mother had been complaining about her knee pain. I explained to Maria's son that we were not citizens of the Netherlands and were not entitled to such benefits. Another time, my mother wanted to ask Maria where we could buy fabrics, as she planned to sew the tablecloths for my brother's wedding day. Maria, without hesitation, asked her son to take us to the store.

One afternoon, I peeked outside my room's window and observed my mother and Maria. They were lounging in their seats while Maria's cats nestled between them. My mother had tied her white scarf around her head like a headband, letting her olive-colored hair fall freely around her face. She poured milk into her tea and left the cup on the table to cool down to her preferred temperature. She stretched out her bare feet from beneath her ankle-length green dress, soaking them in the warmth of the sunshine. Maria's gray dress mirrored the hue of her curly hair. She took a final drag from her cigarette and firmly stubbed it in the ashtray while exhaling the smoke through her nose. She then lifted the teacup to her lips and took a sip.

They were immersed in their worlds, yet they kept each other company in silence.

The scene whisked me back to when I was twelve years old, reminding me of the night when Ali *agha*, Mr. Ali, called me from his backyard, seeking an escape from his haunting loneliness.

*

Ali *agha* was our next-door neighbor in Tehran. He was in his eighties and owned the house adjacent to our apartment complex, which was more or less the same age as he. His house stood like a resilient gem among the few remaining structures that had resisted the land buyers' efforts to replace them with towering high-rises in northern Tehran.

From my room's balcony, I could see his backyard and the porch, where four meticulously carved stone columns lent their support to the ceiling. The crafted wooden door and the tall Orsi windows, adorned with wooden frames and colorful glass panels, bestowed the house with a unique character.

However, the passage of time had left its mark, as if a gentle dust of aging had been scattered upon the house, much like it had upon Ali *agha* himself.

If I didn't know that Ali a*gha* lived there, the backyard would have resembled an abandoned place. The only living creature in the yard was a persimmon tree that somehow clung to life. I often would observe Ali *agha* as he drew water from the well in the corner of his backyard using a black rubber bucket and carefully watered the tree.

The persimmon tree stood tall, reaching ten meters high. In late spring, it turned into a dense cloak of foliage, concealing bell-shaped yellow flowers among its leaves. As fall arrived, the large, oval leaves transformed into a stunning yellow-green palette, and its orange fruits dangled like radiant ornaments.

"I think the persimmon tree is like 'the last leaf' for Ali *agha*," I once told my mother, watching Ali *agha*'s thin body moving around the yard, carrying the bucket of water.

Having read O. Henry's short story, I couldn't help but think that the persimmon tree gave Ali *agha* the will to live, just as the last leaf did for the ill woman in the story.

"It sure is," my mother confirmed.

My mother would often offer him cooked meals. She would call out to him from the balcony, and he would climb up the ladder to reach our balcony and receive the food. Ali *agha* rarely spoke, but he found a way to express his deep gratitude to my mother every fall.

When the tree bore its ripe fruit, he would pluck the persimmons and collect them in baskets scattered throughout his yard. One of those baskets would always find its way to our balcony.

During the last summer of his life, Ali *agha* battled throat cancer, making eating and swallowing extremely difficult. He had lost his strength to climb up the ladder to reach our balcony, so my mother tied a rope to the balcony rods and hung a bucket at the end. She would fill it with ice cubes, the only thing Ali *agha* could eat to soothe his throat pain, and send it down to him. Every hour, he would come under the balcony and call out to my mom, asking for ice.

One night, as I lay on my bed listening to music on the radio, a faint sound from the balcony caught my attention. It was after midnight, and peering into the darkness, I couldn't see anything. I lowered the radio volume and heard Ali *agha*'s faint voice calling my name.

I jumped out of bed and rushed to the balcony. There he was, standing in his backyard, looking up at me. His silhouette under the dim moonlight resembled a fragile skeleton.

"I heard the music. I thought you were awake," he said with his raspy voice.

"Yes, Ali *agha*, I'm awake. Do you want some ice?" I asked, concerned about his painful throat.

He nodded.

As I grabbed some ice cubes from the freezer, my eyes stuck on the bucket of vanilla ice cream. Back on the balcony, I put the ice into the bucket and carefully lowered it to Ali *agha*. He took the ice cubes, looked up, and nodded to thank me. There was something in his eyes, more than a pain in his throat. It seemed he didn't want to return to his house.

"Ali *agha*, do you want some ice cream?" I asked.

He smiled, a smile I had never seen on him before. He nodded like a small boy.

I tiptoed to the kitchen, grabbed two bowls and spoons, served the ice cream, and added a generous spoonful of sour cherry jam on top. Careful not to wake anyone, I returned to my room and offered the ice cream to Ali *agha*.

He sat on the ground of his backyard, leaning against the weathered wall, while I perched on the cool balcony floor above. Not a single word passed between us. We delved into our ice cream bowls, savoring each spoonful.

Ali *agha* shared his loneliness with me that night. Though just a twelve-year-old girl, I sensed he needed my company, even in silence.

Ali *agha* passed away peacefully in his house a few days later. His house was demolished by the end of the year, and the persimmon tree immediately dried up. I realized I was wrong; Ali *agha* had been "the last leaf" for the persimmon tree.

*

I grew up in a large extended family, surrounded by seven aunts and uncles and twenty-five cousins. I also had many friends from school, music, and sports classes. There was always someone to talk to, play with, and exercise with. However, after immigration, I lost most of my human interactions. First, virtual chats replaced physical ones, and then the time difference reduced these chats to messages of congratulations and condolences during significant events. Eventually, interactions were limited to hitting the Like icon on each other's Facebook or Instagram posts.

Building new connections takes time and energy, and I was eager to put in the effort in my new land. I began volunteering at the museums, participating in local public events at the library, and gradually forming new relationships. But my father's arrest caused me to suspend all my social activities, isolating me in a way I had never experienced.

Advocating for my father was an exhausting challenge. I had to work tirelessly on his case without seeing immediate results. Months would pass, and nothing would change despite all the letters, campaigns, and petitions. I had to keep up my spirits and be patient; otherwise, I couldn't continue. I knew this from my father's first arrest, and I had decided to advocate for him with this knowledge. However, I had overlooked an important aspect: I faced it alone this time here in Canada, unlike the last time, when friends and family had surrounded us in Iran.

I had Aydin by my side, but he had so much on his plate. While I focused on my advocacy activities, he would work long hours, often twelve to fifteen hours a day, to support us financially. He would leave home before sunrise, and when he returned in the evenings, he was so exhausted that he'd often pass out on the couch before even eating dinner. He would refuse to go to bed early, wanting to spend time with me, even if it meant sleeping on the couch beside me.

I began to grow fragile from the emotional burden of my father's imprisonment and the challenges of being a new immigrant. At times, the gut-wrenching pain of loneliness would paralyze me, and I felt trapped in a dark hole. It was like leprosy, corroding the soul instead of the skin. It swallowed my inner self, leaving a deep emptiness that felt impossible to fill. The need to escape the pain was overwhelming—and yet, just when I was on the brink of losing all hope, a human connection would reach out and pull me from that suffocating hole.

One of those moments took place a few weeks after I returned from Amsterdam. I had developed lower back pain due to long hours of sitting and lack of exercise. I initially ignored it, but I went to a walking clinic when I realized I couldn't walk for more than ten minutes.

The doctor examined my back and prescribed me an anti-inflammatory medication. As she was leaving the examining room, she hesitated for a moment. She turned back and asked, "Are you okay?"

A long silence filled the room. I stared at the doctor's face, her blue eyes surrounded by wrinkles. Tears slid down my cheeks. I shook my head, unable to find the words.

I wasn't okay. Every day, I watched my husband crumble under his workload. He never complained, but I could see the gray hair appearing at his temples, the weight he was losing, and the dark circles forming under his eyes. I could do nothing to lighten his burden.

I had also received news that my mother, upon her return to Iran, had developed thyroid cancer and needed surgery. For obvious reasons, I couldn't return to Iran to be with her. On top of everything, my father's health was also deteriorating in prison; his arms would go numb from time to time, and he had lost consciousness once. Despite all my advocacy efforts, I could not get him the medical attention he desperately needed. I felt like I was sinking into a dark hole.

I hadn't shared any of this with the doctor, yet she seemed to sense a pain in me that went far beyond physical discomfort.

Dr. Susan stepped back from the door and leaned toward me, her hand resting gently on my shoulder. "Can you wait here for half an hour? My shift will end, and I'll come back to talk with you," she said. I nodded, unable to speak.

She returned after her shift and spent two hours of her own time assessing my mental health and listening to me. She might not have known it, but that day, she was my last leaf—the spark of strength I needed to keep moving forward.

A few weeks later, I undertook the most daunting task of my advocacy. I filed a complaint against the Iranian government with the Working Group on Arbitrary Detention at the Office of the United Nations High Commissioner for Human Rights. With no background in law, I spent countless hours studying national and international law to prepare the complaint—an effort which would not have been possible without the resilience Dr. Susan helped me find that day.

Human connections came to me in various forms throughout all those months of advocating for my father: an unexpected hug from a stranger who saw me in tears on a park bench, heartfelt emails from individuals who had read my father's story and offered their solidarity, a neighbor's simple act of sharing a dish of food, or the kindness of someone helping with my flat tire.

Like Ali *agha* and my mother, I came to treasure these moments, no matter how small they seemed. I realized that while completely filling the void of loneliness might be impossible, these human connections served as a wellspring of strength, helping me not only survive the darkest moments but also find the courage to keep fighting.

THE FOUNTAIN PEN*

I remember how hypnotizing it was as a child, watching my father's pen scribbling on paper. He is among the last generation of writers that still uses a pen on a sheet of paper.

"Typing is soulless," he says.

Writing, for him, is a process of thinking, planning, and creating, which all happen at once as he gently moves his pen across paper. All you can see is a steady movement with no haste and no pause. His pen moves like a pendulum as he engraves the words.

My father is addicted to writing. But more than that, he's addicted to his fountain pens. He writes serious materials, but when you look at them, it is as if he has written a romantic poem. His writings would be short on something without that elegant trace of ink on the paper.

As a kid, I enjoyed observing how he patiently filled the reservoir with black or blue ink. He then drew some lines on the paper, letting the ink flow into the solid-gold nib, and prepared the pen for a long writing. I would sit next to him, imitating his gesture. He gave me one of his broken pens, and I would doodle on paper for hours till I ended up with inky hands and face. He always told me, "One day, you'll become a writer."

On the first day of elementary school, he gave me a diary and asked me to write daily. I did, even though I barely knew the alphabet. In third grade, he bought me a fountain pen for my birthday. Finally, I could have one of my own! I felt I'd

* An excerpt of this story was published in *The Globe and Mail*, December 2019.

grown up and climbed from the first writing step to the tenth. It was such an empowering feeling. The joy of writing with my fountain pen made me write more and more. I would write daily: in classes, during breaks, on my school bus, and in my bed at night. I cared less what I wrote, a diary, short story, or poem, than I did about enjoying the feeling of scribing the words on paper with my fountain pen.

I was twelve when one of my essays was shortlisted for a UNESCO contest. It was about a garden, in our neighborhood, filled with hundreds of trees. Over two months, all the trees were cut down to make way for a towering skyscraper. I wrote about the devastating loss of this green space, a haven for birds, and the harsh reality of its replacement by cold, lifeless concrete. I titled the essay "The Cement Tree" to capture the stark contrast between what was destroyed and what was built in its place.

Later, *Salaam* newspaper, the most-read daily newspaper in the country at the time, published my essay. My father came home with a copy of the paper that afternoon.

"You should start archiving your published writings," he said, and he handed me the paper with a new kind of smile that I translated as, *I'm proud of you.*

I knelt on the living room carpet and opened the newspaper wide in front of me. The sour smell of ink and paper rushed into my nose. I carefully turned pages till I saw my essay's title big and bold at the top of the page, with my name in a smaller font beneath it. I touched my name and told myself, "I am a writer."

For a while, my routine before going to bed was to look at and read my essay in that newspaper. I think I never got over it until other stories and essays were published later.

Back then, the only writer I knew was my father, and I thought having a fountain pen was a fundamental element of being a writer. As I grew up, like any other kid of my generation, I looked for easiness and comfort and used ballpoint pens. Ultimately, I started typing on the computer.

My father, though, has always resisted typing. He had me type out his work until I refused. Since then, he has paid someone to type for him. I bet he's spent more money having his writings typed than he's earned from publishing them. Most of his writings and books have been banned in Iran.

*

A few days after my father's first arrest in 2001, I found my mother crouched in front of his bookshelves, pulling out some books. There were boxes half-filled with books in the middle of the room and many more books scattered around them.

When my mother saw my curious face, she said, "These books are banned. Shouldn't be found here. Otherwise, they might add more charges to your dad." She was afraid that security agents would raid our home and find them.

"Do you throw them away?" I asked.

"No, dear. I store them somewhere else, outside our home," she said. Then she sat crossed-legged on the floor and carefully put the books into boxes.

I was a teenage girl at the time, with a big dream of becoming a writer. I was an avid reader, too. I read whatever I found on my father's bookshelves, from romantic novels to historical and political books. Until that moment, no one had imposed restrictions on my choices of reading material or writing topics. However, my father's arrest served as a jolting realization that in my country, I didn't have freedom of expression.

My father endured an agonizing six months locked away in solitary confinement. He was cut off from the outside world and prohibited from writing, reading, and even visiting his family. He was accused of subversion and was under severe psychological pressure to give a false confession and accept the charge.

It was a tough time not only for him but for me as well.

The only means through which I could unburden the

unbearable pain and distress that suffocated me was the power of the written word. Almost every night, I secluded myself in my room and wrote a letter to my father about the happenings at home, school, and around the country as well as my activities, dreams, and feelings—almost everything. It allowed me to transcend the physical confines that bound my father, bridging the distance between us.

I would use my fountain pen to write the letters. It had been quite some time since I last held it, but at that moment, the fountain pen served as a secret language between my father and me. The ink would flow onto the page, and I would feel his presence as I penned each word.

I had a fear of intelligence agents raiding our home, confiscating my letters, and using them against my father. So, I would conceal my letters behind the frozen meats and vegetables in the freezer.

After my father was released, I gave him the letters. I vividly remember the surprise on his face. He read them within a day or two, and for years afterward, he urged me to publish them as a book. However, for two decades, my desire was to keep them private. Whenever he brought the subject, I would respond, "I wrote them for you, *Baba*."

Solitary confinement had changed my father. Beyond the noticeable physical change—he lost ten kilograms in just six months—something deeper affected him. Beneath his pale skin and forced smiles, he carried a burden. He slept less and wrote more. He sat at his desk day and night for an entire year, pouring his thoughts onto paper, resulting in a six hundred-page book. Although the book never made it to publication, it undeniably brought healing to my father.

The second time he was imprisoned, in 2015, he was held in a public ward where he had access to pen and paper. My mother visited him once a week through a glass partition, and every few months, they were able to meet face to face in the prison's visitation room, alongside other prisoners and their families. During these visits, my mother brought him food and snacks, but all he asked for was his fountain pen.

For months he would complain about the low-quality ballpoint pens he bought from the prison shop: "They are dry, scratchy, and make my fingers sore."

My mother brought his fountain pen several times, but the prison guards would refuse to give it to him. "There might be drugs smuggled in the barrel," they would say. My mother was unsuccessful in convincing the guards that my father was a writer, not a drug trafficker.

I can't blame the guards for their skepticism. After all, my father was detained in a ward primarily occupied by drug traffickers. Although there was a specific ward for political prisoners at Evin Prison, the authorities placed him in that ward with the intention of humiliating and isolating him. However, my father found a silver lining even in such a bleak situation. The drug traffickers smuggled their drugs in, and they showed him how to smuggle his writings out of the prison without them being read or confiscated by the prison authorities.

Finally, my mother reached her limit. She did what she believed was my father's right: She personally delivered the fountain pen to him. She called me after one of these face-to-face visits.

"I managed to sneak in a fountain pen today," she whispered, her voice barely audible.

The words echoed in my mind, filling me with a rush of curiosity and wonder. *How did you do it?* I wanted to ask, but I didn't, afraid that the ever-watchful intelligent agents could overhear our conversation.

My mother changed the subject with a sudden shift, diverting our attention to the neighbor's newborn child. The fountain pen remained unspoken. But my thoughts consumed me, picturing my father's reaction upon receiving that precious gift. I imagined his eyes widening, the creases on his forehead deepening as a smile of astonishment graced his face.

Whenever my mother sent me my father's writings, I tried to imagine how he felt when he wrote them. His pen divulged part of him through his writings. I could feel the soul that existed in his words when he'd been furious, anxious, hopeful, excited, lonely, or worried. I knew where he'd paused to relax his grip on the pen. I felt the pain in his writer's bump that had built up on his right middle finger, at the knuckle below the nail. I would have never sensed all this if he had typed instead.

My father could occasionally call me from the prison. In one call, he asked me what I'd written recently.

I paused for a second and said, "Baba, I can't write anymore."

After immigration, I wrote less and less until I eventually stopped. I was trapped between languages and identities so that I could write neither in Farsi nor English. I would stare at the screen all day without a word typed. My mind was paralyzed. At one point, I thought to myself, *Fine. That's it. My dream of being a writer ended here. I should accept it and move on.*

But my father didn't believe that. "The storyteller in you never dies. You can't stop just because you've changed your place of living or your language," he said. "Look at me! I am in prison now because of my writing. Should I stop?"

I felt an immense sense of shame at that moment. I was sitting in my comfortable living room, enjoying the cool air from the air conditioner, complaining about my immigration problems. Meanwhile, my father endured the oppressive heat and filth of his cell, where the broken water cooler provided no relief on hot summer days, and there was no escape from the bedbugs' bites at night.

He shared a twenty-square-meter cell with twenty-eight other prisoners, real criminals. Eighteen of them were pirates of the Arabian Sea. There were only six three-bunk beds available for all of them, meaning that ten prisoners, including my father, had to sleep on the floor in the hallways and *hossainiya*, a religious congregation hall.

"Prisoners sleep everywhere," my father described to me once on the phone. "Even close to the toilets, packed like sardine conserve."

The conditions within the prison were appalling. There were only five toilets and showers for over two hundred prisoners. The inmates had to wait in long lines and take turns, often without the luxury of warm water. Fundamental rights, such as access to proper medical care, were disregarded. The prison clinic suffered from shortages of essential medicines, and prisoners faced significant delays in receiving treatment. Even seeing a general practitioner was a waiting game, while accessing a specialist or dentist could take several agonizing months.

The available food was sparse and mostly inedible. As my father said, fruit was a luxury item there. It was available every ten days in the ward's shop and was of low quality and high price.

After enduring a few months of this living nightmare, my father's health began to deteriorate rapidly. At the age of seventy, he desperately required surgery on his legs. Still, the bureaucratic process within the prison dragged on for almost a year before he was finally granted hospitalization for the procedure. He told me once, "I wonder if we are in a prison or a torture chamber."

The only place my father—a professor for thirty years at the University of Tehran who has spent most of his life behind his desk—could use for studying and writing was the ward's small library, which had a capacity of only fifteen people. It was open five hours a day and had nowhere near enough books to meet the demand. Nevertheless, my father used any opportunity he had to write.

"Put away that laptop. Get yourself a bunch of paper and a good-quality fountain pen. Sit at a desk and write patiently," he said. "Reflect your feelings into your words. Don't worry about your language and mistakes."

"Writing heals your wounds," he continued. "I learned it from you years ago, when you wrote all those letters. After the darkest depths of solitary confinement, your letters breathed courage into my shattered spirit. I promised myself that if my teenage daughter could find solace in writing, how could I not do the same?" His voice was trembling.

Tears welled up in my eyes, streaming down my cheeks.

"The book I wrote after that was born from the power of your words," he said.

His admission touched a tender place within me. Never before had he revealed the profound impact my letters had on him. My father had always been my role model in writing. I aspired to follow in his footsteps, admiring how he navigated life with unwavering determination. But at that moment, he revealed that he had looked at me with the same admiration, wishing to embody the qualities he saw in me.

I promised him I would write.

A few days later, I found myself sitting at my desk, a blank piece of paper before me and a fountain pen in my hand. It had been a decade since I had last written on paper. The weight of a fountain pen in my hand, the touch of the pen against the surface, and the flow of the ink brought me a familiar sensation I had long missed. It reminded me of those nights I spent writing letters to my father with my fountain pen.

For the first couple of days, I just doodled and played, reacquainting myself with the motions and flow of the fountain pen. It felt foreign initially, but gradually, I regained my comfort and confidence. And then I wrote a short story in a burst of inspiration. It was far from perfect, littered with grammatical mistakes and other errors, but the act of putting my thoughts onto paper brought me immense relief. It broke the seal that had held back my creativity for far too long.

As I gazed upon the words I had inscribed on the paper,

they seemed to come alive, whispering to me, urging me to write more. At that moment, I thought, *Baba is right—typing is soulless.*

I never chose to leave my motherland willingly. It was a decision imposed upon me. Yearning for freedom, I embarked on this journey, carrying the weight of countless wounds and sorrows. I wanted to forget the past and build up the future. I couldn't. The past clung to me like an ever-present shadow, so I began to write about it.

Each word was a testament to what I had left behind and the ache of being torn from my home. I poured my heart into the pages, exposing the raw emotions of my immigration journey, the sense of displacement, and the struggle between two worlds, two identities. I chose not to forget but instead to write and remember.

It was hard to write down the memories, the traumas, the losses. Yet, I knew that I had to face them, to shatter my heart into a million pieces, if necessary, to move forward. As my father had once done while emerging from solitary confinement, I turned to writing.

It was now spring, seven months after my father had encouraged me to start writing again. Over those months, I'd dedicated myself to refining the letters I had penned during his first detention. I decided to tell the story of my family's resilience in the face of injustice.

"I signed a book contract to publish my letters," I told my father on the phone. For two weeks, I'd eagerly awaited my father's call to share the news.

"Finally, I wrote a book, Baba," I continued. I could sense my father's breath on the other end and held my own, waiting for his reaction.

"I've always known that there is a fighter writer inside you," he said.

His voice was shaky, and perhaps his eyes were teary. He didn't say it, but I knew he was proud of me.

NOWRUZ

Before immigration, my favorite holiday was Nowruz, the Persian New Year. Nowruz marks the precise moment of the spring equinox, the most revered time in the Iranian calendar.

The preparations for Nowruz begin weeks in advance with a thorough house-cleaning. In Farsi, we call it *khāne-takānī*, which translates to "shaking down the house." And believe me, it indeed involves shaking everything in the house. At least, that's how it was in our home, where my mother took charge of the cleaning ritual.

My mother would wash every washable surface, from carpets to walls and windows. She would hoover every nook and cranny of the house, taking extra care to clean each niche. She would empty the kitchen cupboards, thoroughly dust and wash them, change the shelf liners, and then put back everything. Not stopping there, she would change the curtains in every room and look into every wardrobe to find clothes that hadn't been used during the last year and donate them.

Around this time of the year, as you walk through the streets, you can spot the signs of *khāne-takānī* in every house. Colorful carpets drape over balconies, swaying gently in the breeze as people diligently beat the dust from them or allowed them to soak up the sun's warmth after being washed. People lean out of the windows to wash away the winter's dirt while flowerpots behind the windowsills are filled with geraniums and violets.

I enjoyed wandering through the Tajrish Bazaar at this time of year. It was where I could feel the energy and happiness that came with spring's arrival in the city. People bustled around, browsing, haggling, and shopping at the various stalls. They hold onto pastry boxes, gold fishes in plastic bags, colorful hyacinth pots, and bags of nuts, navigating through the crowd to get into the shops.

The sidewalks were bustling with hawkers who spread their wares on the ground, all surrounded by eager customers who were bargaining for cheaper prices. This was the only time authorities would permit the hawkers to sell without worrying about confiscation or fines.

A week before Nowruz, my mother would start cultivating the *sabzeh*, grain sprouts. She would say a prayer and grab a couple of handfuls of grain, such as wheat or lentil, from the bucket, dedicating each fistful to loved ones she had lost.

"This one's for *Aziz Joon*," she'd murmur, mentioning her mother, as she gently let the grains fall into the bowl.

"And this is for Farideh." The next batch would be for her sister.

Over the years, the list of beloved ones who'd departed grew longer, including my Uncle Jamshid and his wife Maryam, my aunt Kobra, and Uncle Naser.

My mother would soak the grains in water for a day, then drain them and spread them over damp cloths in various-shaped dishes. These dishes found their place in front of the living room window, basking in the sunlight. My mother misted the cloth-covered grains daily until green sprouts emerged. She would then remove the cloth and wrap a ribbon around the green sprouts. She kept one dish for our home, brought others to the cemetery the week before Nowruz, and put them on the tombs of beloved ones.

Every year, my mother would devise creative ideas for growing *sabzeh*. One time, she decided to use pinecones as little pots. So, she made my brother and me head to Sa'ee Park to collect loads of pinecones from the ground. We returned home with two big sacks full; we must have gathered fifty or more.

The next day, my mother spent hours gently tucking two to three sprouted wheat grains into the tiny spaces between the cone's scales. Within a couple of days, the wheat sprouts started to grow, stretching outward from the gaps in the cones, giving the pinecones the appearance of miniaturized trees. Everyone who visited our home during that Nowruz received one of these sprouted pinecones as a gift.

Another year, she used a pair of clay jars as cozy homes for the sprouts. She cut a pair of pantyhose in half and carefully stretched each leg over a jar to cover its surface. She secured the top part onto the jar with glue. After spraying water on the pantyhose to help it adhere to the clay jar, she delicately pressed the damp, sticky chia seeds onto the fabric. As these seeds began to sprout, they entwined and spread across the jars' surfaces, creating lush green tapestries.

On the eve of Nowruz, we would set up our *Haft Seen* table with seven symbolic items whose names start with the letter S (pronounced "seen" in Farsi), including *sabzeh*. If we had travel plans during Nowruz, we would set the *Haft Seen* on the table ahead of time, and my mother would put together a smaller *Haft Seen* to bring along on the trip.

As the moment of the equinox approached, whether it was daytime or late into the night and regardless of whether we were on a trip or at home, we would gather around *Haft Seen*, waiting for the exact timing. Once it arrived, we would embrace one another in celebration. My father would give my brother and me new banknotes as Nowruz gifts.

Over the next thirteen days, we would journey from one home to another, visiting relatives, neighbors, and friends. These visits were in order of age. Our rounds would commence at my uncle's place, him being the eldest in the family, then move on to my aunt's and the other uncle's. My parents were the youngest children in their families, so our turn to be visited would be in the second half of the holidays.

As a child, I cherished these holiday visits. Beyond the endless supply of pastries and nuts that I could indulge in without my parents holding me back, there was the delightful aspect of receiving banknotes from everyone as gifts.

When my brother and I began attending school, these thirteen days evolved into our travel time. This holiday fell right in the midst of the school year, granting us the longest break. These trips often took place with a substantial crowd—either with families or friends, with anywhere from ten to forty people.

*

My parents are the most sociable and hospitable people I've ever known. They could befriend anyone, and by the next day, that person would be invited to our home.

Once, my father attended a gathering where Osman Mohammad-Parast, a master *dotar* player, was performing. After the performance, my father approached him, mentioned that my brother and I played the *tanbur* and *daf*—both traditional Iranian instruments—and extended an invitation to our home so that we could meet him. Master Osman graciously accepted, arrived that evening, and ended up staying for three nights at our home. Each night, my parents hosted gatherings, inviting friends to meet him.

Without fail, my parents would invite friends or families over on weekends, and even during the week, our home would see its share of visitors. Sometimes, people would show up at our house uninvited, and sometimes, the visitors would sleep over because it was too late to catch the bus to go to their homes. We had pairs of pajamas for the guests who would sleep over. As I was growing up, our place was practically a guest house.

My parents would welcome everyone, whether invited or not. Our samovar was always ready in the kitchen, with freshly brewed tea in the kettle on top. If the guests dropped by during lunch or dinner, there was always a hot meal to serve them.

I was the complete opposite of my parents. I was not too fond of it when people would show up out of the blue. And I never hesitated to express this sentiment to my parents. "Why don't they just call before coming over? I was in the middle of watching my favorite TV show and had to turn it off," I would complain.

"They're guests. We can't tell them to call ahead," they would reply.

"If, just once, you don't welcome them warmly, they will understand and call ahead next time," I would say. But this argument was always in vain because my parents would consistently greet them with wide smiles and warm hugs.

We would treat the guests at our home with reverence, much like gods in temples. The way we served guests depended on the season. During the colder months, we would start with freshly brewed tea, accompanied by pastries or dates. But on hot summer days, we would prepare cold beverages like sour cherry sherbet or *sekanjebin*, a drink made of honey, vinegar, and grated cucumber. Then came the fruits: melons and watermelons in the summer, and apples, oranges, and pomegranates during colder times. My father would sit at the dining table, patiently removing pomegranate seeds while chatting with the guests, and serve them in bowls to everyone, adding a touch of angelica powder and salt.

After the fruit, we would continue with rounds of tea, offering it repeatedly until the guests no longer desired any.

This strong sense of companionship became a defining aspect of our lives, shaping not only how we welcomed guests into our home but also the fact that my parents didn't like traveling alone. They often organized trips with our extended families or their friends.

Our most significant journey was during Nowruz 1997. My

parents orchestrated a grand adventure to Yazd, in the heart of Iran, where the Kavir and Lut Deserts converge. Accompanied by my parents' friends, the travel party swelled to forty individuals in eight cars. As we drove along the road, it felt like we were a grand procession of a wedding or a funeral.

Mobile phones were nonexistent, so each car was responsible for watching over the car behind it. Drivers would peer into their rearview mirrors, ensuring the vehicle behind them kept pace. If a car needed to pull over or make a pit stop at the gas station, the designated lead car would turn around and follow. This system ensured that no car would be lost or left behind in case of mechanical issues.

Back then, the government transformed schools across all cities in Iran into guest houses during the Nowruz holiday, providing essential amenities like carpets in classrooms and conference halls, refrigerators, and camping stoves. This initiative enabled people to rent school facilities at reasonable rates, offering a more budget-friendly alternative to hotels. However, individuals had to bring their own pillows, mattresses, and sleeping bags.

My father had rented a large conference hall in a Zoroastrian school in Yazd. At the top of the entrance, the Faravahar symbol was prominently displayed, encircled by the fundamental teachings of the Zoroastrian faith: "Good thoughts, good words, good deeds."Inside the hall, the floor was adorned with numerous carpets, each displaying different colors and shapes. Every family selected one carpet as their designated "room." They would then arrange their sleeping bags or mattresses on the carpeted floor to create their sleeping area.

It was hard to handle such a big group. But my father had a smart plan. He split everyone into four groups, ensuring fairness for all ages and genders, and no family members were in the same group. Each group had a job for the day: shopping, cooking, cleaning, and doing the dishes. The next day, we would switch tasks.

A corner of the conference hall was marked out as our dining space. When it was time to eat, a long *sofreh*, tablecloth, would be spread on the carpet. The group in charge of cooking for that day would arrange the *sofreh* and serve the meal. Later, the cleaning team would gather the dirty dishes, carrying them to the sinks in the school's restrooms in the schoolyard for a wash.

There would be a vote for any collective activities, be it deciding our meals or selecting the next sightseeing spot. And every individual, regardless of age, had a voice in these decisions. Throughout the day we would explore the city's attractions, and in the evenings, adults engaged in serious discussions about politics and other matters while we, the children, would play in the schoolyard.

The only problem we faced at that school was the lack of showers, so we had to visit a public bathhouse in the city. My mother had told me that during her childhood, when houses didn't have bathrooms, they would go to public *hammam*. There, people would undress and gather around the warm water pool. My grandmother would hire a *hammam* staff to scrub my mother's and aunt's skin with *sefidab*, an ancient Iranian cleanser used to exfoliate dead skin, while she received a massage from another staff member.

It was my first time experiencing a public bathhouse, but I was relieved that it was modernized, with separate shower rooms. "Thank God I don't have to see other people naked," I said, sharing my relief with my mother.

These trips were more than mere excursions. My parents took the opportunity to teach us life lessons. They nurtured in us the art of socializing with different individuals, the power of teamwork, the importance of embracing diverse perspectives, teaching us how to adapt to limited facilities and cherish the present moment.

Not every Nowruz celebration was filled with joy. There

were difficult times, like when Aunt Farideh passed away after her battle with cancer just a few months before Nowruz, leaving the family in mourning. Yet, even in such moments, this occasion brought everyone together.

In Iran, it is a tradition during Nowruz to visit families who have lost a loved one in the past year. The usual rules of age and seniority don't apply here; instead, the grieving family remains at home, and everyone comes to visit them. This custom not only honors the memory of the departed but also ensures that the bereaved family does not feel alone during this time of year.

Another challenging Nowruz was in 2001. We had plans to travel to Bushehr, in the southern part of Iran, with some friends. But things took a sudden and unexpected turn about a week before Nowruz. My father was arrested during his regular weekly political meetup with his friends. Intelligence agents raided in and took everyone into custody. They were all accused of subversion, a charge that was never verified.

My father and his twenty-one friends were detained in solitary confinement and denied access to lawyers and family visits. The families united and decided to use the Nowruz celebration as a means of protest against the injustice they were facing. Just before the equinox, almost sixty of us gathered behind the door of the Evin Prison, arranged the *Haft Seen* on the ground, and awaited the moment. We prayed, embraced each other, handed out pastries and sweets to passing cars, and told them why we gathered there. That particular Nowruz was unlike any other, marked by pain and hardship. Yet, I found solace in it. Amid all the agony, having familiar faces around brought a sense of comfort.

*

Throughout these years in Canada, I've made an effort to celebrate Nowruz. I have followed the rituals of *khāne-takānī*, cultivating *sabzeh*, setting up the *Haft Seen* on my table, and sitting beside it with Aydin at the moment of the spring equinox. We connect with our families in Iran through a video call. But within the next hour, we return to our regular routines, as if nothing has changed, except for the new year on the calendar—one we barely use anymore.

I've come to realize that what I truly miss isn't simply the alteration of seasons, the trips, the bustling vitality of the bazaar, or even the rituals of cleaning our house. It's the people, their presence, their companionship that painted the true colors of Nowruz, whether in joyful or hard occasions. Those colors have faded for me in Canada; those faces are distant. That's what I ache for—the laughter, the tears, the embrace of those who surrounded me. They are the missing pieces that once completed Nowruz.

AFRICAN VIOLETS AND OTHER PLANTS*

Ever since I can remember, my mother has loved growing plants, and so there have always been two or three large ones, like Norfolk pine and ponytail palm, in the corners of the living room and some small ones, like geraniums, on the windowsills.

It was a challenge for my mother to teem our 127-square-meter apartment with plant life before my brother and I left the nest. But she always managed to match everything together: our small living room, the furniture, and the plants here and there.

Every summer in my childhood, she would transform the balcony in my bedroom into a vegetable garden. She would put up hooks and install shelves and planters to use as much as space she could. She would leave a small path through the containers on the balcony's ground, and for three months, only she was allowed to step out there.

As a child, I loved spending summer afternoons sitting on my bed, looking at my mother beyond the large window to the balcony while she watered and pruned the plants in her garden. She would insert sticks into tomato containers and patiently tie the main stems to the sticks to build support. She would make a wooden trellis against the balcony's only narrow wall to plant zucchini along it. She then would train the vines to climb as they grew. When the flowering started, yellow zucchini blossoms would cover the wall toward the ceiling.

I witnessed my mother's joy when she saw the first evidence

* An excerpt of this story was published in *The Hamilton Spectator*, May 2019.

of baby zucchini, tomatoes, and peppers. I would hear her chit-chat with her plants when she praised them—"You made my day, little red one. I am so proud of you"—and when encouraged them—"Darling, you can do better. Look how the bell pepper grows."

She would call me and show me all the new baby vegetables: "Look, here is another one. Isn't it amazing?" Her heart melted every time like a mother witnessing the first step of her baby or hearing the first word from her mouth.

For two months, our dinner plates would fill with whatever my mother harvested that afternoon: *kookoo kadu* (zucchini frittata), vegetable omelets, cherry tomato salads, *boranee bademjan* (eggplant and yogurt dip), and for sure *dolmeh* (stuffed peppers or tomatoes).

At nights, when I'd find peace in my bed, the summer breeze carried the delicious sweet and sour scent of fresh vegetables into my bedroom and intoxicated me. After all these years, among smells of summer—suntan lotion, salt water and warm sand, freshly mown grass, hot asphalt, watermelon, and vanilla ice cream, to name of few—the scent of tomato leaves is still the most redolent to me of this sunny season.

The spring I finished the sixth grade, *Aziz Joon*, my grandmother, passed away. She lived with us the last seven years of her life, and her sudden disappearance was hard for all of us, but especially for my mother. The following summer, she decided to just plant vine tomatoes in memory of *Aziz Joon*, who loved them. She sowed tomato seeds in all the pots we had in our storage that she would use every summer to create her garden. But she seemed not satisfied with their number.

One morning, I found my mother sitting on the kitchen floor surrounded by tens of small yogurt containers, egg cartons, and half-cut soda bottles.

"Maman, what are you doing?" I asked.

"I need containers to sow more tomato seeds," she said

while poking a hole in the bottom of an old yogurt container with a skewer.

"We already have so many pots on the balcony. There is no more space," I said.

She raised her head and looked at me with her teary eyes. "This is for *Aziz Joon*. Okay? It should be glamorous," she said. And then continued poking holes in other containers.

After a couple of days, when all the seeds had germinated, we found ourselves faced with hundreds of vine tomato plants. It was clear that we couldn't possibly take care of all of them, but my mother had a plan. She began giving them away to neighbors, relatives, and friends. Anyone who came to our home or passed by that summer left with a couple of vine tomato plants. It didn't matter who they were—the building janitor, the repairman who fixed our neighbor's washing machine, the garbage collectors, the census officer—everyone received one or two tomato plants. My mother even sent my brothers' and my friends back to their homes with a plant or two.

She patiently explained to everyone how to transfer the plants into a pot, how to build a support structure using sticks, and how much water and sunlight they would need. "My mother loved vine tomatoes," she said with a heartfelt tone at the end of all the instructions. "When you eat them, please say a prayer for her."

Traditionally, when Iranians want to commemorate a deceased person, they make halva—a sweet paste made of flour, oil, rosewater, and saffron—in large quantities. They distribute the halva among neighbors and relatives, asking for a prayer for the departed. However, my mother desired something more than a fleeting sweet dish that would be consumed and forgotten in an instant. She wanted people to remember her mother as she truly was. That's why she offered something that was fresh and vibrant, something fertile and generous.

That summer, my mother kept the memory of *Aziz Joon*

alive in so many households, and I believe it helped her cope with the grief of her mother's passing. However, it was not the last time she would find solace in gardening.

A decade later, when my brother left home to study in Sweden, my mother began cultivating African violets on a larger scale. She bought some in different ranges of colors, sizes, and leaf forms, then she propagated new ones from the leaves of existing plants. Very soon, all the windowsills were filled with African violets. She changed the arrangement of the furniture in the living room to make more space for her plants. No one has been allowed to draw the curtains open or shut anymore since then—this is her exclusive task. She even sets the thermostat according to her plants' needs.

At one point she decided to build up shelves in front of the living room windows to take advantage of the sunlight and have enough room to grow more and more African violets. She created a nursery. The new leaves in the water were on the top right, the ones newly planted in the soil were on the top left, and the strong, older ones were on the bottom shelves. I suppose during the glory days, there were one hundred or even more African violet pots on these shelves.

My mother has worked as a social worker in NGOs for most of her life. Her focus has been on supporting breadwinner women, providing them with training in new skills, and mentoring them to start their own businesses. This line of work requires her to travel extensively across the country. However, ever since the number of her African violets increased to such an extent, she has made a conscious decision to reduce her trips. The flourishing plants have become so dear to her that she doesn't want to leave them alone, without her there to care for their wellbeing and ensure they receive the attention they deserve.

"Who waters them?" she asks.

My father always volunteers, but she never trusts him in this matter. If she really has to leave home, she makes a schedule for my father: when, how much, and how often her plants should be watered; how much sunlight they need; and what the temperature should be. But it doesn't end there. She regularly calls him and checks if he's following the schedule. She even video calls him to make sure the plants are fine.

Relatives and friends ask my mother for African violets, but she refuses to give them. Whoever knows her admits that she is a generous woman, but when it comes to her African violets, she is not.

Some people get really upset and even say, "You have too many plants. What will happen if you give me one?"

"They are like my children. I can't give them away," my mother says.

If that person is so darling to her, she gives a leaf and patiently explains how to propagate a new plant. But after a few months, they mostly come back with the same complaint: "It didn't turn out like yours. What is the secret?"

"Secret?" she says. "There is no secret. Just take care of them." But there is a secret. My mother has refilled the void left by my brother with growing African violets. She has poured her love for him into her plants.

A year after my brother, I also decided to go abroad for education. I went to France, and when I returned home after two years, I was greeted by a diverse collection of cactuses. My room's windowsills were filled with baby cactuses of various shapes and sizes. My desk, where I used to study and do homework, had transformed into a cactus nursery.

Teasing my mother, I said, "Really? You chose cactus for me?"

"Wait to see how they bloom," she said. And she was right.

I can't compare the beauty of a blooming cactus to any other plant—maybe it's because you are not expecting that harsh plant to have tiny, delicate, and colorful blooms.

When the security agents raided our home, during the struggle with me, some of them shoved into the plant shelves in the living room. I'm unsure exactly what happened, as my memories of those moments are foggy. I couldn't hear or see anything. It wasn't until after the agents left that I noticed the mess.

The pots on the upper shelves had fallen onto the cactuses on the ground behind the shelves and broken their prickly spines. African violets had dropped out of their pots, and their soil splattered all over the ground, resembling the blood of a murdered person.

It was a crime scene.

I was happy that my mother wasn't there to witness what happened to me but, more than that, not to witness that scene. With the help of my father, I cleaned the area and saved as many plants as possible. My mother never said anything about the plants, but in her eyes, I saw how heartbroken she was when she faced her empty shelves and broken cactuses.

Plants, for my mother, are not merely a way of decorating and keeping her home hospitable to guests or for air purification. To her, they are living creatures that listen to her without expectations, filling her loneliness and accompanying her when she needs them. In exchange, she takes care of them with perfection.

A few years before I immigrated to Canada, one of my mother's beloved ponytail palms, which she had named Linda—yes, she gives names to some of her favorite plants—began losing its leaves. She dedicated weeks to trying everything she knew to solve the problem. She changed its pot and soil, provided supplements, and meticulously ensured that the watering and room temperature were optimal. Despite her efforts, nothing seemed to work out.

"It's dying," I told my mother.

"Don't say that," she said and gave me an angry look. Deep down, she knew something bad was happening to Linda, but she was determined not to give up easily.

"Let's go to the botanical garden?" my mother suggested.

"I want a botanist check on Linda."

I wanted to tell her, *Maman, it's just a plant. I'll buy a better one for you.* But when I saw her hazelnut eyes, something held me back.

All the way to the botanical garden, she cradled Linda on her lap, like a sick baby nestled in a mother's arm on the way to a hospital.

"Ma'am, we are not accepting any plants from outside. This is a research center," the receptionist at the botanical garden informed us.

"I'll pay whatever it costs. Please, just ask one of your botanists to check on my plant," my mother pleaded.

"It's not about the money," he replied.

My mother continued to insist while the receptionist remained firm in his denial. I stood there, silently observing the scene, witnessing how my mother fought for the life of her beloved plant. I don't know what changed the receptionist's mind for him to finally accept the idea of talking with his manager. Perhaps he got tired of my mother's persistence or felt pity for her desperation.

"This is not what we do here," the manager told my mother while touching Linda's stem. "We conduct research on our own plant collections."

"I understand. I appreciate it," my mother said. "You know this is more than just a plant."

The manager looked at my mother and nodded. I bet he had never seen anyone like my mother, who cares so deeply for her plants. And that melted his heart. He agreed to take care of Linda.

"Here's what I can do," he said. "I will remove it from the pot, wash its roots, trim off any remaining leaves, and place it gently into damp sand to rest and heal." He looked at my mother to gauge her reaction.

"Okay," my mother said.

"This is the only way to see if it is still alive," the manager explained.

We left the botanical garden without Linda. It was the last time we saw it.

My mother would call the research center weekly to ask about Linda for a month or two. However, she always received the same response: "Nothing has changed in its situation, but it takes time. You need to be patient, Mrs. Rafiee."

During the last call, one of the botanists told her that Linda was not alive anymore and there was nothing that they could do. Although we knew this was coming, the news still saddened my mother. She couldn't hold back her tears as she hung up the phone.

"At least we have its photo," I said, trying to comfort my mother.

Linda had been a part of our home for fifteen years, and its beauty, nestled in the corner of our living room, had been captured in many family pictures. I pulled out some photos from our albums and showed them to my mother. Since then, a photo of me playing the *setar* with Linda proudly standing by my side has found a permanent place on my mother's fridge.

*

After immigration, I was preoccupied with so many things that I never asked about my mother's plants. I cared little about what they were doing. I always imagined our home would remain the same as when I'd left it until my father was released from prison.

Finally, after fifteen months, on September 15, 2016, my father was granted medical furlough and hospitalized to receive the treatment we had fought so desperately for.

This pivotal change occurred just few days after the Working Group on Arbitrary Detention at the Office of the UNHCHR released their decision on the complaint I had submitted months earlier. It was the final straw that broke the camel's back. From the outside, it might have seemed as though all my advocacy efforts over those months had been ignored, but I knew they were building up, piece by piece. And then, finally, they worked.

I don't know how many times I reread the decision; each time, I couldn't hold back my tears when I reached these lines:

[. . .]The deprivation of liberty of Mohammad Hossein Rafiee Fanood was arbitrary, being in contravention of articles 9, 10, 11, 19, 20 and 21 of the UDHR and articles 9, 10, 14, 19, 22 and 25 of the ICCPR . . .

[. . .] Taking into account all the circumstances of the case, especially the risk of harm to Mr. Rafiee's health and physical integrity, the Working Group considers that the adequate remedy would be to release Mr. Rafiee immediately, and accord him an enforceable right to compensation in accordance with article 9(5) of the ICCPR.

That day, many human rights and scientific organizations following my father's case reached out to congratulate me.

"This is one of the most powerful decisions I've ever read from the Working Group on a case," one of them said.

After his surgery and a two-week recovery in the hospital, my father was released on bail and discharged to return home.

Our home was filled with relatives and friends celebrating my father's freedom that night. I called my mother for a video chat, and she turned her mobile phone around the living room so that I could greet everyone there. It was the first time I'd seen the entire living room in the past two years. I was shocked to see plants in every corner, every nook, and on every table. My mother's living room had transformed into an urban jungle. People were sitting among all kinds of plants; some hung from the ceiling, and some almost hit the ceiling.

I spoke to my father with a broad smile, welcoming him home, but I felt a heavy weight in my heart. Seeing all those plants, I realized the immense pain and sorrow my mother had endured without ever complaining.

In those two years, my mother had grown numerous plants in her apartment to fill the void left by her children, who resided on different continents and couldn't be there for her when she needed them the most. She also held on to those plants to make her suffering from my father's unjust imprisonment more bearable. African violets and cactuses were no longer sufficient, so she continued cultivating more and more species.

Now, having lived in Canada for a decade and unable to return to my homeland in Iran, I also have dedicated a corner of my living room to cultivating plants that evoke a sense of familiarity. Among them are African violets, geraniums, *Cyperus alternifolius*, and spider plants—the ones my mother adores.

THE SAMOVAR*

Like many other Iranians, my mother visits the cemetery on the last Friday of the year, right before Nowruz, to honor her deceased loved ones. She brings hyacinth bouquets in a rainbow of colors and *sabzeh* to lay on the tombs.

The last Nowruz I was in Iran, I drove my mother to the cemetery. That was in March 2014, and even then, I hadn't visited my grandmother's tomb for several years. That year, I had a feeling it was time.

"I want to say goodbye to *Aziz Joon* before going to Canada," I told my mother. I called my grandmother *Aziz Joon*, a derivation of *Aziz-e jaan*, a Farsi term of endearment that can be loosely translated as "dear to my life."

At the cemetery, my mother squatted beside *Aziz Joon*'s grave, took a small pebble from the ground, and tapped it on her tombstone. "Mother, I've come," she said. "Look who is here too!"

Tears slid down my mother's cheeks. I squatted beside her, laid my index finger on the tombstone, and, like my mother, whispered a prayer.

The cemetery was deserted, perhaps because it was so early in the morning. I heard a *caw caw* not far away, and when I looked up, I saw a crow high in a pine tree, and there, beneath the tree, two women sitting beside a tomb, their faces hidden by their black chadors. From the shudder of their shoulders, I guessed that they were crying and their grief was still fresh.

* An excerpt of this story was published in *Room Magazine*, 2022.

I helped my mother to rinse *Aziz Joon*'s tombstone with a bucket of water. As I poured the water, she rubbed the surface with her right hand. I watched her gentle movements. It was as if she were washing her mother's face. Pressing with her fingers, she wiped the dirt off the name engraved on the stone, and *Aziz Joon*'s name shone in the rays of the rising sun: "Bilqis Khajevand," and, in brackets, "Behjat."

My grandmother had been named after the queen of Sheba, Bilqis. But when she married my grandfather, he called her Behjat, which means happiness. She was the woman who'd brought joy and pleasure to his wretched life.

My grandfather was a highly educated man for his time. He graduated from Dar ul-Funun, the first modern institution of higher learning in Iran. He spoke French and was the manager of a post office in Tehran. I never met him, but when I look at his photos, I can see that he was tall and sturdy, a handsome man. He had a look about him. He had money and prestige. He seemed an ideal man for any woman. Even so, things had gone terribly wrong in his personal life. He had been married twice, and both wives had died childless. People would talk behind his back, saying he was under a spell that had killed his wives. By the time he was in his late thirties, and twice widowed, he was considered bad luck. No one at his social level was about to let their daughter become his third victim.

Then the mother of a girl he'd courted told him to marry a naïve and ordinary girl and divorce her after a month, to break the spell. This would be the only way, she told him, that she'd let her daughter marry him.

It sounds like a fairy tale, but that's what happened.

My grandfather found *Aziz Joon*, a beautiful, so-called ordinary girl half his age. He married her, but when the month was up and it came time to leave her, he couldn't bring himself to do so. He was in love.

A photo of my grandparents in my mother's room dates

to their first months of marriage. *Aziz Joon* stands shoulder to shoulder with my grandfather. She too is tall and slim. Her eighteen-year-old face is so pure, with large hazel eyes and a bony nose. A polka-dot chador is draped over her hair. Is she shy? She seems so, from the way she holds the edge of her chador so that it covers part of her face. My grandfather stands with his shoulders back and chin up, in a European-style suit and peaked Pahlavi hat. A smile breaks out beneath his thick mustache. It's clear he was delighted to have her by his side.

After cleaning the tombstone, my mother poured a bottle of rose water over it. The smell of rose infused in the air, reminding me of the smell of my grandmother's prayer mat. I closed my eyes and envisioned *Aziz Joon* in her floral chador, saying her prayers, my five-year-old self sitting on her prayer mat playing with her amber rosary. She would gently push me away, showing me how to prostrate, and I imitated her right away.

We were inseparable, she and I. We lived in two houses facing each other, separated only by a big courtyard, and she would take care of me during the day while Mohammad was at school and my parents worked. Together, she and I cleaned, played, knitted, gardened, and cooked. *Aziz Joon* was a great cook who made everything from scratch, cleaning, peeling, cutting, and cooking vegetables; making all sorts of pickles, jams, yogurt, and cheese. The smell of her stews simmering in the stockpot and the taste of her golden *tahdig*—a crispy layer of rice that clung to the bottom of pot—are alive still somewhere in my memories.

On nights when I couldn't sleep, I would grab my favorite fluffy duvet and tiptoe quietly down the stairs, careful not to wake my parents so I would not be sent back to bed, then close my eyes and run as fast as I could through the courtyard toward *Aziz Joon*'s house. The sound of wind blowing through the leaves of the eucalyptus tree and the shadows of the branches waving in the moonlight scared me to death. But they would never stop me. I would bang with my fist on my grandmother's window—I wasn't yet able to open the door, and when *Aziz Joon* opened it, she'd say, "Velkeleh, you are still awake?"

She called me this after one of the characters in her stories. Velkeleh was a girl who avoided sleep to protect her siblings from a giant in the jungle who stole sleeping children.

I would find my place under her *korsi*—a short, square table with a heater underneath, covered with a heavy patchwork quilt my grandmother had made from worn-out clothes. One of our games with my cousins was to find our clothing fragments in that quilt. Those with more fabric in the quilt would claim that *Aziz Joon* loved them more.

I would settle into a cozy, comfy spot and wait, and she would bring me a glass of warm milk with biscuits. Then she would start telling me a story: "*Yeki bud, yeki nabud*," which roughly translates to, "Once there was one, and once there wasn't one," our version of "Once upon a time."

I don't know if it was her fairytale-like marriage or something else that made my grandmother a great storyteller. She was illiterate until the age of fifty, but she could spin a story like a bestselling author. There was a magic in her voice that kept me spellbound.

My mother never had that magic. She would read books to me, but *Aziz Joon* would tell stories from her heart, from her soul. These are two different things, and my mother knew it. That was why, when we moved to England for my father's studies, my mother had *Aziz Joon* record her voice on cassette tapes. She knew that *Aziz Joon*'s voice and stories would be the one place where my brother and I would take refuge night after night in a foreign land.

I could never sleep while *Aziz Joon* told me stories. My eyes glued to her lips, I was all ears till she would say, "*Ghesse-ye maa be sar resid, kalagheh be khoonash naresid*"—"And so hereby ends our tale, and the crow didn't get to its lair."

"Why didn't crow get to its lair?"

"Because he has more stories to tell before going home."

Then she would turn off the lights and put her hands over my eyes. Eventually, I would fall asleep beneath the roughness of her fingers, and tucked under the *korsi*, I would dream about the stories.

My grandmother never ran out of stories, be they mythical or mystical, humorous or actual historical events. Not all of her stories were fairytales and happy endings, either. She had dark stories, which my mother wasn't happy about. She would tell *Aziz Joon* not to tell these stories, but when my mother was not around, *Aziz Joon* spun stories of betrayal, hatred, and enmity. A friend kills another friend because of greed; a son leaves behind a mother because his lover has lied; a father abandons his children in the jungle because of a jealous stepmother.

With no happy ending, I would get sad sometimes. "Why did this happen?" I would ask. "I don't like the ending."

"Life is not always fair, honey. You should know that," was her answer.

*

Those summers were a lot of fun. They began with *Aziz Joon* moving two king-size wooden beds out of storage and placing them beside each other in a corner of the yard. She covered them with a Persian carpet, thin mattresses, and cushions to make it comfortable for her guests to sit and lean back against the yard's thick brick walls. In the afternoons, when the sun's strength began to wane, she would water the garden and get ready to host her neighbors. The afternoon breeze mixed with the freshly watered plants to make a pleasant environment that no air conditioning could compete with.

Aziz Joon would cut watermelons and prepare snacks of cheese and bread. Then came my favorite part: when she prepared her Russian samovar. She began by placing lighted charcoals in the vertical pipe to heat the water in the brass bowl. When the charcoal was glowing steadily and the water boiling, she would place the samovar on a silver tray at the corner of the great bed in the yard, to the right of where she herself would sit. Then she'd put two spoons of tea leaves in a porcelain teapot, add cardamom, rose flowers, or chamomile, and fill the pot with boiling water. The pot was then placed on the top of the samovar, to brew the tea.

Her neighbors would show up one by one, each with something to do during the visit. Some afternoons they bought kilos of mixed herbs, like mint, parsley, dill, cilantro, and tarragon, and they would trim the stems and chop them while chatting. Other days they peeled twenty kilos of eggplants or trimmed and chopped green beans. From time to time, when they'd take a break, *Aziz Joon* would serve tea with pastries, snacks, and watermelon.

On the afternoon they broke sugarloaves, *Aziz Joon* would spread out a clean cloth on the beds and set out tens of tall, conical sugarloaves shaped like snowy mountain peaks.

"*Besmellah*"—in the name of God—Marzi *khanoom*, our next-door neighbor, said. Taking the first sugarloaf, she would break it into pieces with a hammer.

The other women would then use their sugar nips to break the pieces into sugar cubes. In minutes, our courtyard was filled with the sounds of breaking sugarloaves and women's chattering. Clouds of dusting sugar would fly all about, the yard as sweet-smelling as a confectionary shop.

I would sit cross-legged beside *Aziz Joon* and dip my fingers into the pile of dusting sugar, and when nobody noticed, I'd lick my sweetened fingers one by one.

On this day, *Aziz Joon* would serve only tea. "A scalding tea is just the ticket," she would say. Pouring freshly brewed tea from the teapot into a thin-waist glass on a saucer, she would gauge the color of tea and adjust its strength by adding boiling water from the samovar. When the tea was perfect, she would pass it to her guests.

My other entertainment was to watch how everyone drank their tea. Each had her own style. Some, like Marzi *khanoom*, would ask *Aziz Joon* for a darker, stronger tea. Marzi *khanoom* wouldn't wait until that tea cooled off. Her hennaed nails would lift a sugar cube off the cloth and put it between her teeth, then she'd slurp the hot tea in delight. I wouldn't take my eyes off her mouth till the sugar cube melted slowly as she took the second and third sips.

Mrs. Zahedi, by contrast, liked light tea. She would dive into the pile of sugar cubes, push some away with the back of her fingers, and, selecting the biggest one she could find, bite down on it to cut it and get just the right amount. Then she'd raise her glass to her lips, and sip through the sugar cube fragment. And so on, for the next sip.

Aziz Joon tended to pour tea into the saucer to let it cool off, then dip a sugar cube in the tea and drink straight from the saucer. Like all other things, I would imitate her way of drinking, but instead of melting the sugar in the saucer, I kept the cube inside my mouth. I liked the way it sizzled slightly when I placed it on my tongue. Then I'd slurp my tea from the saucer, and with each sip, another sliver of the sugar melted.

At the end of the day, the women would pack up the sugar, dust off their clothes, wash their faces and hands in the yard basin, and leave with their share of sugar cubes.

"Now, bring all the sugar cube bowls," *Aziz Joon* would instruct me.

So, I'd run all over the two houses and grab the sugar bowls to fill with the remaining cubes. All the while, *Aziz Joon* would be cleaning the samovar to make it ready for next day.

When I was six, our lives changed dramatically. We sold our and *Aziz Joon*'s houses and moved into a three-bedroom apartment. The courtyard, garden, summer afternoons with the charcoal samovar, and winter nights under the *korsi* all disappeared. *Aziz Joon* came to live with us and became my roommate. I didn't understand why all the changes, but I couldn't ask for anything better than to sleep head-to-head with my grandmother and drink in her stories every night.

Aziz Joon, though, was not so happy. Once I found her sitting by the window, watching the pouring rain.

"I've missed the sound of rain falling on the roof and dripping from gutter," she said. We lived on the first floor of the building and could hardly notice the downpour.

She would miss her home of many years. Since marrying, she had lived in that house. All her children had been born and grown up there. She held their wedding ceremonies in its courtyard. Her grandchildren grew up playing there. She knew everyone in that neighborhood. The baker, the butcher, the greengrocer all called her by name, Behjat *khanoom*. And now, that whole world was gone.

The samovar was also not so lucky. It became another decoration in our living room. Every Nowruz, my mother would disconnect its parts, dab a glob of tomato paste on its brass surface, and wipe the tarnish off. Then she would put the gleaming samovar back together again, for it to sit as décor until the next year.

For three decades, the samovar sat dormant.

*

My mother came to visit me in Canada in the spring of 2018. My father couldn't join her, as he was barred from leaving Iran. Although more than a year had passed since his release from prison, his case remained open. This is a common tactic of the judicial system when dealing with political activists: they release them on bail but keep their cases unresolved, using this as leverage to monitor their activities and easily send them back to prison if needed.

My mother arrived with suitcases brimming with love in the form of food: sweets and savories, bags of nuts, chopped herbs for stews, fried eggplant, and more. I had told her not to bring a thing.

"What's this?" I asked when I found an irregular-shaped package under clothes, buried in her luggage.

"*Aziz Joon*'s samovar," she said. "She left it for you. It's in her will."

"I know. But what can I do with it?" I said, trying to unwrap the odd-shaped package.

"Put it somewhere as a decoration," my mother said, looking around. "How about there?" She pointed to a corner of the kitchen.

I shrugged unwillingly.

"Is this still functioning?" Aydin asked.

"It should be," my mother said. She sounded doubtful. "We haven't tried it for years."

A few days later, we tried to use the samovar in our backyard. In addition to the samovar, my mother had packed thin-waist glasses with saucers, a porcelain teapot with painted roses, and its matching sugar bowl. Sitting in the backyard, gazing at my grandmother's treasured samovar after all these years, hearing the sound of boiling water and smelling the rose flowers in the brewing tea, I felt something happening in my heart. I couldn't put it into words.

Aydin and my mother sat chatting, but I wasn't listening to them. My body was there, but my soul was somewhere in the distant past.

Taking a sugar cube, I set it inside my mouth, poured tea into the saucer, and blew on it like *Aziz Joon* would do. Then I took a sip, and I was five years old again, sitting beside *Aziz Joon* on the great wooden beds in the open courtyard, drinking tea, my face and hair covered with dusting sugar.

I had lost so many things with my immigration. I'd felt my broken heart would never heal. But in that moment, sipping tea again with my grandmother's samovar, I felt a piece of my heart come back to me.

Everything might be gone, I thought. *Aziz Joon, motherland, and home, but their memories, love, and spirit will live through me.*

Now I take the great brass samovar to every picnic and barbeque. The first thing my friends say is, "Don't forget to pack the samovar." It is the heart of our outdoor gatherings in Canada, like it was for *Aziz Joon* and her friends.

When my nephew, Sahand, was born in 2019, I digitized the stories on *Aziz Joon*'s cassette tapes, thirty-five years after they were first recorded. I sent my present to my brother's newborn. "A gift from *Aziz Joon*," I wrote on the CD.

AM I MY PASSPORT?

"Have you seen Niagara Falls?" all my friends and family kept asking me when I came to Canada. And they didn't stop until I sent them photos.

"Me and The Niagara Falls," I texted.

The first and only thing we learned about Canada at school in Iran was that Niagara Falls is the largest waterfall, by volume, in North America. For Iranians, it is the symbol of Canada. Not the maple leaf, not the beaver. So, when my brother Mohammad came to visit me in the fall of 2017, the first place I took him was the Falls.

Aydin and I had visited there only once, on Canada Day two years before. The experience was terrible. We ended up swaying in the crowd like a tide swell in the ocean. When we finally got close enough to see the Falls, we were suddenly pushed back until we ended up farther away than ever. We could not enjoy the Falls that day.

This time we decided to go in middle of the week, to escape the crowds. Aydin was driving, following the GPS. Mohammad sat next to him and I was in the back, listening to their conversation about why everything is bigger in Canada compared to Europe. My brother had been living in the Netherlands for a decade. This was his first visit to North America, and he was amazed by the size of the cars, houses, parking spaces, even ketchup containers.

"Everything is big here," he kept saying.

When we arrived in Niagara, the GPS showed that we

should pass a bridge, which I later learned was the Rainbow Bridge. Midway across the bridge, we knew something was not right. There, ahead of us, US Custom and Border Protection officers in dark uniforms were guiding traffic, directing all the vehicles through different lines.

"We are going to America," I said, looking at the big US flag waving in the breeze.

Aydin checked the GPS and found out it was set for Niagara Falls, US. "It's okay," he said calmly. "We make a U-turn."

"I don't have my passport on me," Mohammad said.

I felt sick at my stomach. *This won't end well*, I thought.

Aydin pulled up to the gate.

"Where are you going?" the officer in the booth asked.

"We made a wrong turn. We wanted to go back," explained Aydin with a smile that faded a few seconds later.

"You are on American soil now," the officer said. "Where are you from?"

Aydin hesitated. "I am a permanent resident of Canada," he said. He knew the name Iran would not be welcome.

That January, President Trump had issued his Muslim ban, an executive order that banned travel from several Muslim countries, including Iran. And there we were, three Iranians on American soil.

"Sir," the officer asked, his voice constricting, "what is your nationality?"

"Iranian," Aydin said.

"*All*?" The officer bent slightly and peered inside the car.

"Yes," Aydin said.

"I need to ask you to park your car over there," the officer pointed, "and go upstairs to the second floor."

We climbed the stairs, a long silence between us. *Aydin and I are permanent residents. They might check our IDs and let us go*, I thought. *But what about Mohammad? He is in Canada as a visitor and doesn't have a passport on him. They may arrest him.* I felt apprehensive.

The fresh-faced officer behind the glass partition on the second floor told us that sixty to seventy people make the wrong turn every day. "It's a common mistake here," he said. His smile was comforting.

So, I realized, *it's not just us.*

"They just turn around and go back," he continued. "But, you know"—he paused and looked us up and down. I broke out in a cold sweat from the look. "Because of your nationality, we need to document your entry onto US soil. You know what I mean?" He smiled again.

We all nodded without hesitation, confirming that yes, we knew. What we knew is that Iranians are seen as terrorists, as fundamentalists, as violent criminals. We knew we would be interviewed, photographed, and fingerprinted. We knew we could not do like others who made the same mistake we had and simply turn around and freely return to Canada.

Sitting on a bench, waiting to be called for fingerprinting, I wondered what would be different if I was Canadian. I remembered what my instructor had said on the first day of integration classes: "As a permanent resident, you are like Canadian citizens with just two differences: you don't have a passport and you cannot vote."

Are there really just these two differences? I'd wondered then and wondered again now, as a detainee at the border because of a wrong turn.

By the time I was called, a family of four had come upstairs to see the same desk officer. I saw the blue passports in the father's hand. I could tell from their accent and appearance that they were immigrants as well.

"Where are you going?" the officer asked.

"We are going for a day trip on the US side of Niagara Falls," the father said. "We are Canadian." He handed the passports to the officer. There was a hastiness in that one sentence. As an immigrant and a person of color, I knew our faces said things before our documents did, before our true selves could speak up.

"We need to ask some questions and check your documents." The officer scrutinized the passports.

The mother set her two kids on a bench in front of us and gave them snacks. She then approached her husband and stood next to him. They looked in each other's eyes and did not exchange a word. My heart sank at that look. How familiar was the frustration and anxiety in their eyes!

"Maryam," a deep voice called out. A burly officer asked me to follow him to a room in the back of the office. He was tall, almost double my height; he might have been sixty or so, clean-cut with gray hair and light skin.

"I'm going to take your photo and then scan your fingerprints." He talked without making any eye contact.

I nodded and followed his instructions. First, he took my photo. Then, I stood in front of the scanner on his left side. He grabbed my right hand. I felt the heat pass through the blue rubber gloves he wore.

It was a sunny day. The temperature inside the building was mild. I had a light jacket on, and I wasn't feeling cold. But my hands were frozen, as if I'd just pulled them out of a bucket of ice.

Am I scared?, I asked myself.

He pressed my thumb on the scanner. "One more time," he murmured. Again he pressed my thumb, and then again. He repeated this three times. He shook his head.

What's wrong?, I wanted to ask but didn't. I was there to obey, not to question.

"Your hands are too dry," he said. He wasn't informing me; he was complaining. He then started rubbing some kind of lotion or cream on my fingertips.

I stood still and watched the officer with that blank look on his face, handling me without even asking my permission. What could I say? I knew there was nothing I could do to stop him. He was on the side of the law, and I was a guilty person who had accidently breached the border, a guilty one who was born in Iran, a guilty one whose skin was too dry.

All I cared about at that moment was getting the fingerprinting done so I could leave that building, leave that soil. I wanted to leave behind those red-and-white-striped flags with stars that stared at me everywhere I looked. I wanted to get back home to a cup of tea. I wanted to stand in the shower and cry, let the water tumble over me and wash all this away.

They held us for a couple of hours while we were each interviewed, photographed, and fingerprinted separately. Finally, our documents were validated by authorities in Canada. We were free to head back across the border.

As we crossed the Rainbow Bridge again, Aydin tried to make fun of what had happened. "You finally went to America," he said.

I gave him a pale smile. "It could be worse," I said. "They could have arrested us."

Mohammad and Aydin nodded.

"They were respectful," Aydin said. And Mohammad and I nodded.

My eyes were glued to Canadian flags flying in the air. *I am going home*, I thought. I felt able to breathe again. I could see that Mohammad and Aydin also looked more relaxed, and we finally got to see what we had planned for the day. We stepped out of the car and heard the roaring Falls. We walked along the pathway toward the brink, and the sound got louder and louder. The crowd was not large, and we could stand together in the best spot to enjoy the scene. At least we'd chosen the right day! I looked at Mohammad and Aydin. Both stood in silence, taken by the Falls in all its glory.

I breathed into the rising mist. On my skin I felt the spray from the water crashing onto the rocks. I felt relieved, grateful, secure, and then suddenly incensed. I was confused by all the feelings. Looking at the green flowing river way below and the white foaming water falling freely, I asked myself, *Was I treated respectfully at the border?*

*

A month after the border incident, I took a drawing class at an art gallery, thinking I would entertain myself during the long, gloomy winter. The first day of class, everyone introduced themselves by talking about their favorite artists and why they were taking the class. These were casual introductions to break the ice.

"I am Nathalie. I am an art teacher," the woman opposite me said. Her eyes looked young. She was perhaps in her early thirties, but the silver highlights in her hair gave her an older look.

"Who is your favorite painter?" our instructor, Kevin, asked.

"I like Monet," Nathalie said, "the way he used color and light in his paintings."

Kevin nodded and turned his face toward the next person, who introduced herself and then said, "Ever since I saw *The Scream*, I've been a fan of Edvard Munch."

Monet? Munch? I repeated the names in my head. *How illiterate I am in painting*, I thought. *I need to google all these names tonight.*

The class was arranged in a U-shape, with Nathalie at one tip of the U and me at the other. Kevin was standing in the middle, facing each person who talked. At the beginning, I could only really see his back, then his profile, until suddenly I found him staring at me.

My turn, I told myself. I felt uneasy. Not because I didn't know much about the painters. There were others like me who'd passed on naming any artists. I realized I did not know what to say.

The silence was long enough that Kevin raised an eyebrow.

"My name is Maryam," I said. I held back, looking at the faces staring at me. More silence. I could hear the hurried breathing of the old man a few seats away.

Kevin took one step toward me. Perhaps to encourage me, to get me to continue.

"I am an immigrant," I blurted.

How weird was that, not just for me but for the rest of the class? No one wanted to know about my background any more than I wanted to know about theirs. *Why did I say that?*

After class, I challenged myself to find the answer. "Something is wrong about it," I told Aydin over dinner. "When people introduce themselves, they say, 'I am a doctor,' or, 'I am a teacher,' not, 'I am an immigrant.'"

"It's fine," he said. "Don't think about it."

But I would think about it. For days. And I began to notice something. Whenever I was in a situation where I had to introduce myself, I would mention that I was an immigrant to explain that if I had an accent or looked different, it was because *I am not from here.* I would do it especially around white Canadians, like that night in painting class. Why was I always doing this? Was it because I didn't feel that I fit in, so I would sort myself into a category where I actually belonged? And the best was the category of "immigrant"—or was it just the safest?

Realizing this was shocking. My whole life had been one escape after another from being slotted into this or that category, or submitting to a label. Now I was using "immigrant" to define myself in Canadian society. Why? Did I think people might mistake me for someone else, someone unfamiliar to them? My face, my name, and my accent would reveal me as an immigrant. No one would think otherwise, and yet I was confessing to people all the time, like I needed to be the one to say it first. Or was I just trying to say who they wanted me to be? I had accepted the role written for me by others—I was stereotyping myself.

That is what happened at the US border. I was who the officer had wanted me to be: an Iranian, a danger to American soil, someone who needed to be questioned, fingerprinted, photographed, documented. I was not treated respectfully at all. I was treated like a criminal. And the painful part, I realized, was that I believed that day that all of that was normal. I was even thankful I hadn't been arrested.

What has happened to me? I asked myself, but no answer came. That's when I started to dig, really dig into my memories and traumas. The change hadn't happened in a day or two. There was a history behind the change. I had opened old wounds I couldn't close, and now I needed to explore them.

*

The experience of not belonging started early in my life. I was born a few years after the 1979 revolution. Schools, like other institutions, would promote Islamic values that restricted girls especially.

I can still quote my teachers' lengthy speeches about how to be a "good Muslim girl," covering hair and body from *namahram*—the men with whom marriage was generally permissible. Such a girl would say her prayers on time, not laugh loudly in public, and not question the inequality between boys and girls.

"If you don't wear hijab or say your prayers, you will burn in the hell." I heard this line a million times.

This was at a time when even having a VHS player or a satellite TV was forbidden, meaning that people could only watch national TV, which promotes the state's values. At school, we were questioned about whether we had the banned devices at home, and what we were watching. We were questioned about the books, magazines, and newspapers our parents read. Did they drink alcohol? Did they go to Friday prayers?

From the time I was seven years old, I knew things were different in our home. While my classmates visited their grandparents and played with their cousins on the weekends, I spent time with my parents at their political meetings. I understood their talk was different from what I learned at school or heard on national TV. And I knew I shouldn't discuss these meetings or my parents' activities. If I said what they did at school or read or watched, I knew that would hurt my family.

I never fit the definition of a Muslim girl that school imposed on me. I was a happy girl who liked to cycle in the streets and laugh out loud in public if something struck me as funny. To bear the restrictions, I found my escape by dreaming. While reciting my rituals along with my peers, I lost myself in a world of daydreams during the mandatory noontime *jama'ah* prayer at school. I envisioned myself as an archaeologist in ancient cities, an environmentalist exploring deep caves, or a cyclist competing in a race.

As I bent and stood in imitation during the prayer, I would imagine myself in shorts and skirts wherever I went, with my hair flowing freely in the air, unrestrained by the mandatory hijab. When the prayer concluded, I eagerly anticipated the following day, when I would continue where I'd left off in my dreams.

As I grew, society's restrictions grew as well. A Muslim girl was not safe being out after sunset, could not travel alone, and was not allowed to have a boyfriend. I found that I was forbidden to watch football matches in a stadium and sing in a band. The list of restrictions never ended. Then, instead of dreaming of a fairer world, I started to learn about the world outside, where women were free and had the same rights as men.

Two incidents were helpful in this learning process as I became a teenager. The first was when the state removed the ban on VHS players, which led to the opening of rental shops that carried Western movies—censored, of course, which I cared little about. Mohammad and I would go to the rental place near our house, choose the movie we wanted to watch, and, along with paying the rental fee, we had to leave one of our birth certificates as a deposit to ensure we returned the VHS. At the time, VHS movies were rare and the technology to copy them was not easily accessible, so the store manager wanted to ensure he got his tapes back. The movies such as *Jurassic Park*, *E.T.*, *Scream*, *Mrs. Doubtfire*, *Dead Poets Society*, and *Forrest Gump*, to name a few, revealed a world parallel to the one I was living in—very different, but fascinating.

The second important incident was when Mr. Shaparaki became my English teacher at the private Language Institute, where I studied English twice a week. It was the first time a man had been my teacher, and his perspective on girls and life was transformative. Mr. Shaparaki grew up in a boarding school in England, and I believe this experience made him a different man and a unique teacher. He liked to empower girls and encouraged us to be fearless in following our dreams.

On one occasion, he shared the story of his marriage to his former classmate. "There was a cockroach in the classroom, and everyone was screaming and climbing onto the stools," he said. "But Toofan walked straight toward the cockroach, calmly killed it with her foot, picked it up with a tissue, and threw it in the trash without a trace of fear." He paused, his expression softening as the memory washed over him. "At that moment, I fell in love with her," he added.

This was a different narrative from what we were usually told: that women should be humble and keep their heads down to attract men. Here was a man telling us that he admired a courageous and self-confident woman.

During one conversation in class, Mr. Shaparaki learned that I would play *daf* and then asked me to bring it to class and perform. "The sound is loud. The office will scold me," I said.

"Don't worry about the office. I will deal with them," he encouraged me.

At that time, even carrying an instrument in public was challenging, let alone playing it. My father would put mine and my brother's instruments in the car's trunk to keep them out of sight and take us to our music class. I never told my friends or teachers at school that I played an instrument, to avoid the judgment of not being seen as a good Muslim girl. But Mr. Shaparaki's insistence compelled me to bring my instrument to English class. At the end of the class session, he arranged the benches in a circle like a theater and asked me to perform. It was my first time playing the *daf* for an audience beyond my family. He created an experience of my being heard and seen as an artist publicly.

Mr. Shaparaki would often talk about his experiences with cooking, as his wife didn't like to cook. I had never seen a man publicly share his interest in cooking. Once, he gave us a recipe for his favorite pasta. "It's simple: Chop the garlic and fry it in olive oil. Then immerse the boiled pasta in the oil, stir, and grate some cheese," he said. When I got home, I tried his recipe, and since that day, it has been my favorite pasta recipe, even after three decades.

Every summer he would have a week-long family reunion in a different European city. Once, he went to Barcelona, and when he returned, he regaled us with stories of the city's nightlife—how people danced in the streets and music was everywhere, even after midnight. I couldn't even imagine this scene. The only nighttime scene I was familiar with in Tehran streets involved Basijis—members of a paramilitary volunteer militia—setting up roadblocks, stopping cars, and questioning where people were going and why they were out in the middle of the night.

Mr. Shaparaki was not just an English teacher; he was a life teacher who showed us that real life extends beyond the dos and don'ts imposed by society. He encouraged us not to be afraid to break taboos and labels. He taught us that we didn't need to follow the role models created for us and that we could be ourselves.

The Western movies and Mr. Shaparaki's stories made me feel like a stranger in my country. I felt that I could not fit in there. I longed to explore the Western world, to see what democracy looked like, how people lived in freedom. I thought that in that world, I could truly be myself—free from dos and don'ts, labels, and categories. I imagined a place where I could define who I was without distorting myself to fit in.

In 2009, I went to France for my master's studies and experienced freedoms I had never had—freedom of thought, freedom of expression. I could wear what I wanted. I could be friends with anyone I wanted and go wherever I wanted. I thought I could finally fit in *and* be myself.

Then, a few months into my studies, when one of my research posters was accepted by a conference in the US, I tried to get a visa. It was a Monday morning when I arrived at the US embassy in Paris, a huge hall with windows all around. I sat on one of the benches in the middle of the hall, waiting to be called. Looking around, listening randomly to the conversations between officers and applicants, I could tell that most of the conversations were friendly. People even sometimes laughed.

"Oh, you're going on vacation? Where?" asked one officer.

"Hawaii," answered the applicant.

"Great," the officer said. "Your visa will be ready in the afternoon."

This is not so bad, I thought. But after three hours of waiting, I grew nervous. People had come and gone, and I was still there, waiting for someone to call my name. I checked my documents. My conference invitation, my university acceptance, my bank statement, my full scholarship from the European Union to study for my master's—all that, plus my research paper, was in order. So why the wait? Don't worry, I told myself, there is no reason to be rejected—you are more than qualified.

Two more hours passed. It was nearly 2 p.m. when I heard my name.

I reached the stall to find an overweight officer frowning at the papers in his hand.

"Hi," I said and heard nothing in response. When he raised his head and looked into my eyes, I said "Hi" again.

He did not answer. Instead, he asked, "Why do you want to go to the US?"

How can I explain the tone? The tone was like, *How dare you apply for a visa to the United States?*

I took a deep breath and began explaining that there was this conference, and so on and so forth. As I spoke, I passed the documents to the officer through the small opening in the glass partition.

"Where did you learn English?" he barked.

What? Is that important? "In Iran," I said. I was speaking to this man who seemed to frown the entire time. When I talked, he stared into my eyes, but his eyes would steal away when he asked a question. He asked about my parents. He asked about my brother—what they did, where they studied, where they lived, and so on.

"What does your father think about the future of Iran?"

I was stumped. What should I say? Was there even a right way to answer? "My father is a political dissident, but he is optimistic about the future," I finally said.

No relief came. Instead, there were more questions. "Why did your brother choose Sweden? Why he is studying physics?"

I felt uneasy. I just wanted to present a poster at a conference about preserving cultural heritage, and here I was having to explain my family history, the thinking of my family members, why they had chosen this or that route for their lives. Just like in childhood, I was being interrogated by some authority figure, only this time, I didn't know what was wrong or right to say. So, instead of guessing, I told the truth.

The officer got up and left.

I had a bitter taste in my throat. I felt something wasn't right. I looked around the hall. It was deserted. There was only an Asian man in a black suit on the far side of the hall talking to an officer.

After another half an hour, even the Asian man left.

Finally, the officer returned. I could tell from his face where this was headed. First, he passed back all the documents. He made no eye contact with me. Then, the verdict I already knew: "You know," he said, now staring at me, "we can't give you a visa."

I had a lump in my throat. Six agonizing hours in, I was hungry and thirsty. I was tired. I hadn't even used the washroom the whole day, fearing that my name would be called and I'd be absent. I had been interrogated, and now they were rejecting me. Tears slid down my cheeks. I could not control them.

When I looked at the officer's name tag to call him by his name, I saw that he had turned it around so I couldn't see it. I didn't know who had questioned me, whether he even had the right to ask me all he did.

"Why?" I croaked.

"You know," he deflected, "you speak English very well."

What? Is it the reason? "This is not fair" were the only words I could get out.

"You know," he said, "you are young. You can go to the US later in your life. Just not now," he added.

I don't know. Stop saying "you know." I wanted to yell at Officer No-Name. "I know you rejected me," I said, "because I am an Iranian. It is more respectful to just say this." I don't know how I managed to spill out all those words without crying.

"*No, no,*" he said, to my astonishment. "It is not about your nationality."

But in his face, something had changed. I knew he knew that he was talking nonsense. He had that superior look on his face, that *I-know-who-you-are* look, that *just-submit-to-what-I-tell-you* look.

I felt defeated. It was no use. I couldn't talk any more. I slipped into the embassy's washroom and cried and cried. My heart was broken. I gathered toilet paper for my runny nose. I sat there for I don't know how long and vented.

I left the embassy with red eyes and a swollen face.

The night before, I had checked the map and found out that the US embassy was very close to the Champs-Élysées. Just a five-minute walk away. This was my second time in Paris, and I'd planned for my first experience of the Champs-Élysées. I had a plan to walk the world's most beautiful avenue, look for a nice café, sit in a row of tiny round tables facing outward, order my coffee, and take all the time I needed just to people-watch. And perhaps make small talk with those around me, or exchange some smiles while relaxing on this iconic avenue, like all the people I had watched in the movies.

I sat instead on a bench beyond the grove of trees that line the Champs-Élysées. I wanted to hide from people. I took out my passport and stared at it. I felt belittled and humiliated. I realized my nationality—really, the burgundy passport in my hand—would define me. Outside the borders of my motherland, I was a potential terrorist. Even in a democratic country, I would be categorized, slotted, detained. I would not be who I was. *I am my passport*, I told myself, feeling again that I did not belong—not there, not anywhere, not really.

When the time came to get a visa for other countries, I ran into the same dead end again and again and again. Ireland, Italy, the Netherlands, Canada, the list never ended.

*

In 2019, when I got my Canadian citizenship, I slipped away from work for an hour to go to the ceremony. This was in middle of the week, and when I got back to work afterwards, some of my colleagues congratulated me.

One of them asked, "How do you feel now as a Canadian?"

I was flustered. I didn't know what to say. *What I am feeling?* I asked myself. *Am I happy?* Yes, I was happy, because finally I would be seen as a worthy person in a world. *Am I sad*? Yes, I was sad, because I had been worthy before this ceremony. The difference was that I was ignored then.

I said none of this to my colleague. What I said was, "Nothing special."

Two years earlier, I would have told her I was happy to be here and to be Canadian. But those revealing experiences at the border and in the drawing class had changed me. I had come to Canada to be free of labels, not to fit into new ones. So, I had decided not to be what people wanted me to be and not to explain myself if I didn't want to, or accept things because people thought I should. I reminded myself of what Mr. Shaparaki had taught me: not to be afraid to be myself and not to follow the models created for me by the society.

This change has been hard. It's hard on people like my colleague, who give me weird looks and stop talking to me after saying, *You're not grateful for what you have and where you're living*.

What they do not know is that I have been doing my best to be who I want to be, not who others want me to be.

A few months after the ceremony, I was invited to speak at the University of Tennessee in Chattanooga about my newly published book and my advocacy work for my father. Since his release, I'd started volunteering to share my experience at student advocacy seminars held at various universities in partnership with Scholars at Risk. Once, their efforts had helped my father, and now I wanted to give back. In my speeches, I encouraged students to continue their advocacy work by highlighting how essential their efforts were in keeping hope alive for individuals facing unjust imprisonment.

At Pearson Airport in Toronto, I handed over my Canadian passport to the US officer. It was my first trip as a new Canadian citizen. I stared hard at the officer's face, perhaps searching for a familiar gesture, a frown. He only asked simple questions about where I would stay and what I would do in the US.

I walked toward the boarding lounge with the strangest feeling. I had never been treated like a normal human in such a situation before.

I sat on the bolted benches and tried to digest my experience. I looked at the blue passport in my hand. *Am I my passport?* I asked myself. I was as confused as I'd been a decade ago on the Champs-Élysées.

At the end of my talk at the university, one of the students asked, "How can we become more responsible towards human rights? And help people like your father?"

I paused to reflect. I scanned the room filled with a hundred first-year students. The students stared at me curiously, looking for an answer. I felt my heart beating faster. *They are the future*, I told myself.

"Don't be like politicians who build walls, let some people in, and keep some out," I said. "Stop judging people based on their nationalities, sex, color, religion, gender, ideology." I stepped forward on the stage, wanting to tell them something more important. "Don't categorize people. Don't use geographical borders to define the people living inside them."

I could hear my voice, and it was shaking.

THE PANDEMIC*

I was five or so, standing in a line with my mother for rationed butter and sugar on a sizzling-hot summer day. Butter had been out of stock for months, and I hadn't had my favorite breakfast for so long that I had forgotten how it even tasted.

"Maman," I said, "can I have honey and butter with bread tomorrow morning?"

"Sure, darling," she said. "We'll get the butter today, and we'll have a delicious breakfast." Her smile was reassuring.

The designated store was far from our house. People went there from all parts of the city. We had no other choice. You couldn't simply drop by the supermarket close to home and get the rationed items. My mother used a newspaper to fan me and herself. Another woman in the line fainted, and people asked for water to revive her.

After hours in line, we finally got two sticks of butter and a kilo of sugar. We took a taxi home. Looking out the taxi window, I watched the streets of Tehran, war-torn, windows crisscrossed with duct tapes, sandbags stacked against walls, and young soldiers marching off to war. My attention was still mostly on the next morning's breakfast.

"*We got the butter, we got the butter*," I sang as we entered the house.

My brother ran into the room. "Where is it?" he asked.

My mother opened the plastic bag to put the butter in the fridge, and when she did, we realized it had melted. An oily

* An excerpt of this story was published in The Ex-Puritan, 2022.

mess streamed out of the packages and all over the plastic bag.

My brother's smile faded. He stood by the kitchen door, not moving.

My mother knelt on the floor, the oily mess covering her hands. Then she broke into tears. "Sorry, baby," she said.

I hugged her and stroked her hair. "It's okay, Maman. Please don't cry." I could smell the butter. It smelled delicious.

I was born in the middle of the Iran–Iraq war, a war that began in 1980 and lasted eight years. During the war and for years after, people would stand in line for hours with their ration coupons to buy essential food and goods. Sugar, rice, meat, cheese, oil, tea, and other commodities were in short supply. Whenever the government would announce that it was time to go and claim a specific product at a specific store, people would skip class, cancel appointments, or ask for time off from work, then rush to the designated stores with the ration coupon in hand. People would stand patiently in line, sometimes for a whole day, in the sun or rain. It could be a heatwave, it could be storming.

Supplies were scarce. No one knew when essentials would be available again. Every other day, my mother would leave home early in the morning to get a place in line to buy our share of milk. Two bottles. The distribution truck would arrive at the supermarket just after sunrise, and there was no guarantee that people waiting at the end of the line would get their milk.

When I was ten and my mother had hand surgery, getting the milk fell to my father, who already had a lot on his plate: work, hospital visits, my brother and me. He had no time to stand in line for milk. He explained our family situation to the supermarket owner and asked him to set aside the bottles that he could pick up after work. The owner agreed—for double the price.

During those long years, electricity was also rationed. For hours at a time, blackouts would occur throughout the country, one region after another. Kerosene heaters were the main source of heat for most households during the winter, only kerosene was scarce like everything else. In the cold Tehran winters, people would stand in endless lines, in deep snow, holding portable cans, waiting on their refills. I can still see them, covered in snowflakes, blowing on their hands, rubbing them together, shifting from foot to foot, just trying to get warm.

Filling a prescription was another story. Most of the time, people couldn't find heart pills for their grandmothers or cough syrup for their kids. People would go all over the city, from one pharmacy to the other, to find the medicine they needed, or go to the black market and pay ten times the original price.

As the years went on, the memories of the wartorn Tehran of my childhood faded somewhat. But the Covid-19 pandemic brought them back. I saw scenes I thought I would never see again, especially not in Canada: shortages, empty shelves; long lines at grocery stores, banks, and supermarkets; cancelled flights, deserted streets, panicked eyes, and the constant news of death. It was similar to what I'd lived through during the war.

"Can you believe I stood in a line yesterday to enter Costco?" one of my colleagues said during our break. She took a sip of coffee before continuing, "This is the craziest thing." It was mid-March 2020. The pandemic had just started.

"During my childhood, people stood in line for almost everything," I said to comfort her. "It's not a big deal." Her blue eyes grew wider, still sipping her coffee, with a look asking, *Where on earth did you grow up?*

A few days into the pandemic, I realized that my Canadian colleagues were panicking more than those of us who had lived through wars or economic sanctions. People here had lived a peaceful, privileged life for so long in their democracy, far from war, famine, forced lockdowns, or any kind of shortage, that they felt their lives change dramatically. It was being called a war against the virus.

"I just can't believe it," I heard people say. "This feels so unreal, like an apocalypse movie."

I watched my colleagues go out at lunchtime to look for sanitizer and toilet paper. They would come back with the information. "No masks or sanitizer in any pharmacy, but you can have one pack of toilet paper per person at Shoppers."

My Iraqi and Syrian colleagues and I would listen and nod our heads in sympathy, but we were not panicked, especially not about toilet paper.

"Do people get diarrhea from coronavirus in the West?" one of my cousins asked our family group chat, followed by a laughing emoji. He then shared photos of people fighting over toilet paper in England.

"What do you do with that much toilet paper? Do you want me to post some packs?" another cousin teased those of us in Western countries. "Let's make a YouTube tutorial video of Iranian toilets to show Western people that they can wash themselves with water," he wrote.

Every toilet in Iran has a hose attached to a water valve behind the toilet so that you can easily wash yourself. Easy and practical.

"You might go viral with that video," I wrote to my cousin in the group chat.

I did not stockpile groceries. I wasn't scared when I faced empty shelves. But I got angry when I couldn't cook *sabzi polo mahi*—herbed rice with fish—our traditional dish made for Nowruz. There was no fish at the grocery store.

"What are they thinking?" I asked Aydin. "Is famine coming to Canada?"

My immigration experience helped me cope with things that were unfamiliar to many Westerners. For most Canadians, the notion of virtual attendance at their loved one's birthdays, weddings, and funerals was novel but also weird. My immigrant friends and I had been doing that for years. When two of my uncles died during my early years in Canada, I could not take part in their funerals. When four of my cousins got married, all I saw were their spouses' pictures on social media. Two of them have babies, and I have no idea what they look like. My mother takes videos for me at weddings and birthday parties, and sometimes I have video calls with my extended family, although the time difference between Tehran and Ontario makes that hard.

Since immigrating, I've had a virtual family. My mother's worsening heart disease, which progressed with age, made it impossible for her to endure the twenty-hour journey from Tehran to Toronto. Meanwhile, my father was barred from leaving the country. The pandemic didn't change this reality, but it deepened my suffering and intensified the pain of separation and loss.

Early on, Iran became a hot spot where the virus spiraled out of control. Due to the economic sanctions, there was no PPE and there weren't enough ventilators. Many people lost their lives every day. I was terrified because I had parents in their mid-seventies. I would call twice a day to check if they were okay. "Please stay home," I would beg them hundreds of times.

"Don't go shopping."

"Eat whatever you have at home."

"Are you coughing? Do you have a fever?" I would ask whenever I heard my mother clearing her voice.

I had a breakdown when one of my mother's friends passed away from the coronavirus. It happened so fast. I would cry every night and wonder what I would do if something happened to my parents. I felt guilty that I couldn't take care of them.

*

In April 2020, we moved to another city because of Aydin's job. We had planned for this move months before, not knowing that a pandemic would turn our lives upside down. Suddenly, we couldn't hire movers or ask for help from friends. It fell to the two of us to move the queen-size mattress and the two-hundred-pound dining table. It took half a day to load the rental truck and another half a day to unload it. The following day, my muscles were sore and trembling. Aydin's fingers were so swollen that he couldn't even open a jar. We rested most of the morning. It was late afternoon when I slowly started to unpack.

At 7 p.m., I heard loud noises outside the apartment. It started with a cheer, a woman's voice from the far side of the building. Then other voices joined in, howling, cheering, clapping.

"What is it?" I asked.

"I think people are thanking the healthcare workers," Aydin said.

I rushed out to the balcony and started clapping. It was chilly out, and I was barefoot on the cold cement, but I didn't care. I didn't want to miss the moment.

The sound of whistles caught my attention, and I saw two women dancing in the visitor parking lot, cheering up the neighbors, whistling along, all while keeping socially distant, two meters apart. Grabbing the balcony rail, I stretched my neck out—something I would never do normally —and saw my new neighbors to the right banging pots and pans with wooden spatulas. We nodded and smiled at each other. More heads started appearing out of windows in the opposite building, and more neighbors started howling and waving at us. One person had a walker. She waved and then had to grab it quickly to keep her balance before she could wave again. I waved back.

Some car alarms went off in the parking lot. The beeping made for a noisy ending to that Friday evening.

A moment before, I had been moaning in pain and cursing my bad luck. Then, all of a sudden, I was cheerful, clapping and howling. I felt better when I stepped back inside. That joyful ruckus was more than just a thank you to healthcare workers. It lifted my spirits. It reminded me that I was not alone in this pandemic. It reminded me that there were so many others like me, people who'd lost loved ones, who couldn't see their parents, and who were worried about them day and night.

That was collaborative therapy, and it worked better for me than other therapies did. Standing on my balcony in Burlington, I realized that this feeling wasn't new; it brought back memories from a decade earlier, on my rooftop in Tehran.

*

In June of 2009, a controversial presidential election took place in Iran. The results were rigged, the ruling regime appointed their favorite candidate as president, and the people pushed back. Massive protests broke out throughout the country, and it became known as the Green Movement. People marched peacefully in the streets, holding up signs that read, "Where is my vote?"

The authorities retaliated violently, hitting, arresting, and killing people. Armed forces and heavy vehicles filled the streets to disperse any "crowd" of more than two. People were ashen-faced and speechless. Terror and horror were everywhere. Still, people found a way to deal with their fear, grief, and anger. Every night at 9 p.m., when darkness fell, people would go to their rooftops and shout, "*Allahu Akbar.*" God is great. As soon as the first voice pierced the quiet of the night, more voices would join in. The cries of "God is great! God is great! God is great!" echoed across the city.

People found ways to show their solidarity by taking advantage of the protective darkness that shielded their identities. This was not a new concept to Iranians. My parent's generation had used the same tactics during the 1979 revolution, when the Shah was killing protesters in the streets. However, this was new for me and soon became a ritual. I would knock on my neighbors' doors in my apartment building to call them out to the rooftop, where together we would shout "*Allahu Akbar*." Then we would pause. There was a moment of silence that would be broken by voices from the building across the street. They would reply to us and then wait. "*Allahu Akbar*," another rooftop would cry. This was like a code between us, meaning we were together in this catastrophic situation.

We stayed on our rooftops for an hour every night, venting our anger and sadness about what was happening in the country by shouting and crying. But more than that, we did it to show that we had each other's backs no matter what. It gave us hope. I would hardly have a voice the next morning. But come nightfall, I would do it all again.

Then, the security forces cracked down on us. They would identify the houses and buildings from which the cries of "*Allahu Akbar*" came by marking the doors with black or white spray paint. The following morning, they would raid those buildings and arrest people. This never happened to any house or building in my neighborhood, though, thanks to Mr. Tamjid, an artist in his late seventies living in my apartment building. He never came up to the rooftops, but every morning before sunrise, he would go around and paint out the marks on the doors. I would see him every morning when I was leaving for university.

"You can go to the rooftop tonight," he would say. "I took care of the marks." Then he would disappear into our building with his paint bucket and brush.

During my youth, I watched as an oppressive system tried to isolate and frighten people. Now, the oppressor was a tiny virus. It might not be the same, but it felt similar. Then, I didn't know what would happen to democracy and freedom in Iran. Now, I didn't know what the world would look like post-pandemic. Both situations triggered terror, fear, and grief. But from shouting on the rooftops in Iran to cheering and howling on my balcony in Canada, I felt like I was part of something bigger, part of a large group of people who were spreading the message that we need to be unified to overcome hardship.

*

Being from the Middle East—where war and sanctions never stop, where your movement is restrained and your freedom is taken from you—had prepared me for many aspects of living through a global pandemic. It didn't seem like an apocalypse movie to me. The life that Westerners described as abnormal is the reality of countless people in different parts of the world.

People in the West had no sense of what it would be like to live in a situation like that until the pandemic. The pandemic was a glimpse of life in forced lockdowns, life under constant fear of death because of a lack of access to medicine or food. It showed Westerners how it feels to be separated from loved ones without knowing when you will be reunited. Just a glimpse.

I thought the pandemic might have a silver lining when I saw the world united in its determination to fight the virus. I hoped that global solidarity would help end other destructive forces: wars, economic sanctions, and oppressive systems.

I was wrong.

After the pandemic, we've instead witnessed more fuel being poured into war machines, more economic sanctions being imposed, and more refugee crisis being created. Once again, I've been reminded of the divide between "our" lives and problems, and "theirs."

THE WEAKEST PERSON IN THE ROOM

"We are hiring now," the sign read at the entrance of a fancy grocery store. I had passed the sign three times that week, and each time I'd stop and stare at it, thinking, *Should I apply?* I had no retail experience, and cashiering had never been part of my career aspirations, but I had to start somewhere. Almost two years had passed since I'd immigrated to Canada, and despite having two master's degrees, I had failed to find a job.

When I was in my twenties and looking forward to my thirties, I imagined myself as the most successful woman I had ever known. I'd pictured myself living out my true purpose, doing what I was passionate about and excelling in it, making a positive impact on others, and ultimately feeling fulfilled. However, now, here I was in my early thirties, standing in front of a grocery store, contemplating whether to apply for a cashiering position.

Back in high school, I had grand ambitions of becoming a heart surgeon. I had read an article about Doctors Without Borders in the newspaper and felt like I had found my dream job. "It combines two things I want the most: helping people and traveling," I used to tell my parents.

In my dreams, I never envisioned myself in a white, ironed hospital uniform, surrounded by dramatic situations like in *Grey's Anatomy*. Rather, I would immerse myself in images of wartorn regions or disaster-stricken areas. The thought of rescuing helpless people filled me with such profound satisfaction that I couldn't imagine pursuing anything else.

However, this dream came to a sad end when I couldn't pass the entrance exam for medical school at the age of eighteen. Instead, I pursued studies in chemistry. Becoming a chemist wasn't my dream, but I was too young to be bothered by it.

During my undergraduate years, I studied less at school and focused on enjoying life by traveling extensively. As I explored historic sites and immersed myself in the profound heritage of my ancient country, a new dream began to take root within me.

I decided to pursue a career as a conservator of historic buildings. Once again, I could picture myself on scaffolding or perched atop a church or mosque, meticulously repairing and restoring historic tiles and paintings.

Driven by this passion, I pursued not one but two master's degrees in the field of cultural heritage preservation, one from Iran and another from a joint program in Europe. However, reality turned out to be different from my dreams and expectations. In Iran, I faced disappointment as I struggled to find a job. Inefficient management, international sanctions, and economic recession severely impacted the cultural heritage sector, leaving it with no budget, projects, or job opportunities—a situation that seemed to offer no glimmer of hope.

Then Aydin and I decided to immigrate, and the situation worsened. In Canada, I sent out hundreds of résumés but received no response. Not even one.

A friend who had been living in Canada for a decade advised, "You can't secure a good job without a Canadian degree. Consider applying to a college or university here."

Another friend suggested, "Try simplifying or altering your name on your résumé. If employers can't pronounce your name easily, they might not reach out to you."

During my integration classes, my instructor also emphasized the importance of "Canadian experience." "You need

Canadian experience. It doesn't matter if you have a decade of work experience or a PhD degree. Apply for a general job to gain that trust," she said.

Initially, I didn't believe any of these suggestions. With each job application, I reassured myself, *The employer will review my résumé and recognize my qualifications.* My approach was to invest all my efforts into seeking a job in my chosen profession while avoiding general jobs. But I finally gave up.

The application for the cashiering position was smooth. I had an interview with Mrs. H, who would become my supervisor later on. She offered me the job right after the interview, which I accepted with delight.

The next day, Mrs. H took me and another trainee to tour the store.

My first impression was that the store's employees were predominantly white, with only two other cashiers and myself as the exceptions. The rest of the staff were white Canadians. Even the customers were mostly wealthy and white.

"You have three days to look around, learn the product and bulk item names, and memorize their barcodes," Mrs. H said.

The other trainee and I nodded in acceptance, but Mrs. H seemed unsatisfied. She turned her head towards me and added, "I understand you might have some challenges with English, but I believe three days should be sufficient, right?"

What do you mean by "challenges with English"? I wanted to ask, but I didn't. I felt embarrassed in front of the other trainee who was sixteen—half my age. Even before immigrating to Canada, I could communicate in English very well. I had an accent, but I wasn't dumb.

"Three days will be fine," I said. Blood rushed to my face, and I felt my cheeks grow warm.

Later that day, I came out of the women's restroom and bumped into a tall, overweight man. "Who are you?" he asked.

I was momentarily taken aback. *Excuse me! who are you?*

I wondered to myself. He looked familiar, but I couldn't recall where we had met before.

My eyes locked onto his name tag. It was Mr. L, the owner of the store. Suddenly, I remembered seeing his picture above the store entrance—a warm smile on his face, his arms wide open in a welcoming gesture to everyone who entered the store.

"I am Maryam. I just started today," I said, extending my hand for a handshake, but he remained still.

"Nice to meet you," I continued, retracting my hand and feeling uneasy.

He asked, "Where did you park your car?"

"I didn't have a car," I replied.

"Good. If you ever have one, remember to park it in the back spots of the plaza," he said, and then he left.

During my lunch break, I spoke with one of the cashiers about my earlier encounter with Mr. L.

"Did he really tell you where to park?" She raised her eyebrows in surprise. "It's a huge plaza. No one parks in the back. Park wherever you want," she added.

On the first day of my second week, Mrs. H approached me and asked me to close my cash register for the customers. She stood in front of me with some papers in her hands.

"We received some complaints from our loyal customers," she said, looking at the papers.

Did I do something wrong? I thought, feeling flustered.

"They complained that one of our cashiers wouldn't bag their items properly," she said, raising her head from the papers to look at me. "After reviewing the security footage, we realized it was you," she continued.

"Okay," I said, my mind completely paralyzed. I was only in my second week of working at my very first job in Canada, and I was still in the training period.

"Just make sure to do the job right. We are very respectful to our customers," she said.

I nodded, feeling as though I were admitting guilt. Mrs. H smiled and left.

I reopened my cash register and started scanning the next customer's items, all the while thinking to myself that maybe I had done something wrong. However, I couldn't find any wrongdoings in my actions.

The harassment never stopped.

"Why aren't you smiling at the customers?" Mrs. H would say.

I would force a big smile on my face, and by the end of my shifts, my facial muscles would ache.

"Your conveyor belt is dirty, clean it," Mrs. H would order. I would look at the other conveyor belts, and they looked worse, but she wouldn't say anything to the other cashiers.

"Yes, Mrs. H," I'd respond obediently.

Two minutes later, she would yell, "Why are you stalling the customers?"

"I'm just cleaning the conveyor belt, Mrs. H," I would explain.

"You're too slow. Don't you want to keep this job?" she would taunt.

I would grab, scan, and bag. Grab, scan, bag. I would clean the station and conveyor belt. Then, again, grab, scan, bag until I couldn't stand on my feet anymore.

"Don't talk to your colleagues," Mrs. H would demand.

"I was just asking for a barcode for an item," I would defend myself. This was a common action among other cashiers.

"You're lazy and incapable," she would say, continuing her hurtful remarks.

Every week, Mrs. H would test the cashiers to check their performance in remembering the barcodes of grocery items. She would choose around twenty-five to thirty items and time us while we cashed them out. During the three months I worked in that store, I never made more than three mistakes, but she always blamed me for not working hard enough.

"You have to check the items more frequently since you have difficulty with English," she would say. "If you want to work here, you should do your job better."

Determined to prove myself, I worked even harder. I started showing up to work earlier than my actual shifts. I would walk around the grocery section, checking the names and barcodes of the products, practicing and memorizing as much as I could. At home, I diligently wrote down the names and barcodes in my notebook, spending time memorizing them. I wanted to demonstrate that I was smart and deserving of my position.

For so long, I thought all my struggles were my own fault until I accidentally overheard Mrs. H's conversation with two other cashiers. They had seven to ten mistakes in their tests, yet Mrs. H was praising them, saying they did great.

"It's fine. Just make sure to check the items next time to avoid mistakes," she said with a big smile. I don't remember her ever smiling at me, maybe only on the day she interviewed me.

"I want to take revenge," I told Aydin over dinner that night.

"How?" Aydin asked.

"I will quit right before the Super Bowl without notice," I said. "They'll be busy on those days and would be shorthanded."

"If you want to quit, just do it now. You can't change them," Aydin said.

"They treated me like trash. I want to do something that they understand," I said.

*

Two weeks before the Super Bowl, Aydin left behind our apartment key at his work. He texted me that he would come to the store during my break to get my spare key. I came out of the break room with the key in my hand. As I spotted Aydin walking towards me in one of the aisles, I smiled and hurried over to him. But, to my surprise, he looked serious and quietly murmured in Farsi for me to pretend like we didn't know each other as he passed by.

I stood there, puzzled, not knowing what was going on. I wanted to follow Aydin to find out, but just then, Mr. L approached me. He seemed curious and asked if Aydin said something to me.

Confused, I told him, "No. Why?"

Without waiting for my answer, Mr. L rushed off, chasing after Aydin. I was left standing in the middle of the aisle, wondering what had just happened and why Aydin wanted us to act like strangers.

I opened my cash register, but my eyes would follow Aydin's every move. He strolled casually through all the aisles, picking up items, examining them, and then returning them to their shelves. Right behind him was Mr. L, tailing Aydin like an undercover cop on a mission. It was as if Mr. L suspected Aydin of being a shoplifter, waiting for any sign of a crime to occur so he could pounce and catch him red-handed.

"Mrs. H, aisle six. Mrs. H, aisle six," Mr. L's voice echoed over the store's intercom.

This cat-and-mouse game had escalated, becoming even more captivating as Mrs. H joined forces with Mr. L to chase after Aydin. For a good ten minutes, Aydin led them on a wild goose chase throughout the grocery store.

Throughout the whole ordeal, I watched the scene with pure amusement. It was a rare moment of satisfaction in that store, and I relished every second.

Finally, Aydin made his way to my cash register. "Can I have the keys now?" he asked with a mischievous grin.

Handing him the key, I said, "Thank you," unable to hide the happiness radiating from my face.

Mr. L and Mrs. H approached. Mr. L was huffing, beads of

sweat forming on his forehead from the chase.

"Mr. L, Mrs. H, this is my husband, Aydin."

"Oh, really. Why didn't he tell me?" Mr. L retorted, showing no signs of remorse for his actions. It was evident that he had chased Aydin simply because of the color of his skin.

"I wasn't aware that everyone who steps into your store needs to introduce themselves," Aydin replied calmly. "My apologies, next time I'll be sure to do just that," he continued.

I couldn't contain myself. Laughter bubbled up from within me. Aydin twinkled at me, and with a quick nod, he left, leaving Mr. L and Mrs. H standing there, still looking flustered and caught off guard. They resembled two spoiled white cats whose clever little mouse had just slipped through their grasp.

Oh God, how I relish seeing them like this, I thought to myself, unable to wipe the smile off my face.

I quit the grocery store two days before the Super Bowl. And I never stepped into that grocery store again.

"I just want to let you know that this is my last day," I told Mrs. H. She didn't ask why. She knew.

This wasn't my last experience with discrimination in Canada. Over time, I have realized that discriminatory behaviors come in various forms, some obvious, others hidden beneath the surface. But in both cases, when I've chosen to address the discrimination, I've often received responses that aim to diminish its significance, such as a claim of a misunderstanding, an insistence that I misinterpreted the situation, or even a denial of any harmful intent.

These explanations are often accompanied by sympathetic faces, seemingly expressing regret that I've been made to feel this way and undergo such experiences. Yet these sentiments are abruptly overshadowed by the insertion of a conditional *but*.

"I am sorry you feel this way, but it was not what I meant," they would say. This *but* effectively nullifies all the empathetic words that came before it. There should be no room for a *but*.

*

A few months after leaving the grocery store, I started working as a pharmacy assistant. One day, almost at the end of my eight-hour shift, a customer came in to fill a prescription for his son.

While I was filing it into the system, I asked, "When do you want to take it?"

"Aren't you listening to me?" he yelled at me.

I was completely shocked by his reaction.

"I told you it is for my son. I am not taking it," he yelled again.

It hit me that I had used the wrong word—*take* instead of *pick up*.

"I'm sorry. I'm sorry," I said, flustered. "English isn't my first language, and I mixed up the words. I meant to say 'pick up,'" I explained, my voice shaky with nerves.

"First learn how to speak, then come to work!" he yelled. "Fucking immigrants," he muttered in disgust before storming off.

I stood there, frozen behind the computer, my entire body trembling, trying to hold back my tears.

The pharmacist emerged from the counseling room and noticed me in that distressed state. He came over and asked me what had happened.

I attempted to explain, but I ended up bursting into tears and couldn't manage to utter any words. After a couple of minutes, I was finally able to share with him the details of the encounter with the customer who had treated me in a racist manner.

The next day, the pharmacist informed me that he had spoken to the customer when he returned to pick up the medications. The customer had claimed it was all a misunderstanding and that he hadn't meant to be offensive.

"He offended me," I said.

"His son was sick in the hospital, and he was probably exhausted and said something he shouldn't have," the pharmacist said. "He didn't mean it that way," he added.

I didn't say anything else.

*

I began law school in 2021, but the decision of becoming a lawyer wasn't made overnight. After my father's release, everything seemed to be falling into place: I found work in my field, Aydin was thriving in his career, and we had settled in Canada, free from the initial challenges of being new immigrants. Yet I couldn't shake the feeling that something was missing. I wasn't satisfied; I wasn't happy.

When I would share these feelings with my friends, they often reminded me to be more grateful—for my health, my position, my safety, and my freedom. "Do you know how many people want to be in your place?" they'd say.

Those who knew about my father's imprisonment often scolded me too. "Your father is out of prison—what more do you want?" they'd ask.

And in some ways, they were right. My father seemed to have resumed his normal life after prison. He lived with my mother in their small apartment in Damavand, a quiet city outside Tehran, away from the city's air pollution. Their home, as usual, became a hub for family, friends, and neighbors. Whenever I called them, someone was there—no surprise! He also pursued his usual activities. He wrote, used new platforms like Clubhouse to engage in political discussions, and regularly gathered with his friends. A few times, the intelligence agency summoned him for what they called "a talk," merely reminding him that they were monitoring his activities but had no plans to arrest him—yet.

Once, I had believed my father's release would bring me the peace of mind. But it didn't. Even after seven years, I found myself questioning: *Did I make the right choices?*

I couldn't go to the one place I longed for. I was living in exile, unable to return to my homeland, and that suffocated me.

"What is wrong with me?" I asked Aydin one day. "We have a stable job, a roof over our heads, holidays wherever we want—why doesn't any of it make me happy?"

"You've lost your cause," he said. "You're an advocate, a fighter for justice. Sitting in a lab testing samples . . . it's not you."

"Why can't I just be grateful for what I have?" My voice dropped to a whisper. "Maybe I'm depressed."

"I don't think you're depressed," he said. "I've seen you. When you're speaking at advocacy seminars or presenting your book, your whole demeanor changes. There's a spark in your eyes, a fire in your voice. That's when you come alive. Maybe . . . that's what you're missing. That's what you need to pursue."

That conversation ignited something deep within me, a spark I hadn't felt in years. It pushed me to search for a cause that could bring meaning to my life, even in exile. Slowly, I began to see the truth: All the advocacy I had done for my father wasn't an end in itself—it was preparation for something greater. With renewed purpose, I applied to law school, determined to become a human rights lawyer and turn my passion for justice into a lifelong mission.

After a few months in law school, I was at my doctor's office and casually mentioned my move to Toronto for school.

Curiously, my doctor inquired about my area of study, to which I replied, "Law."

"Oh!" she replied, seeming surprised.

"So, what will you become?"

I looked at her, trying to make sure I understood her question. She looked serious in asking it.

I took a moment to gather my thoughts before responding, "I suppose a lawyer."

"I see," she said.

This wasn't my inaugural experience with such reactions.

Some people struggle to envision a Middle Eastern woman with an accent pursuing law and becoming a lawyer. Their reactions and words insinuate that I don't belong in that world. It's not always easy to spot, but this bias persists, even in law school.

A few weeks into my second year of law school, there was a discussion in class about the midterm exam. Initially, our professor had mentioned in the syllabus that it would be a take-home exam due on Friday of week five. However, some students had classes on Friday, so he offered to change it to an assignment to be completed during the reading week. Students shared their opinions both for and against changing the assignment, and he suggested other options, such as having a twenty-four-hour take-home exam on Saturday or a three-hour exam on Friday at 4 p.m.

On that day, I was sitting in the first row, very close to the professor. Like other students, I wanted to share my opinion, especially when he mentioned an exam option at 4 p.m. on Friday.

"I have a class on Friday afternoon," I said.

I intended to explain that writing an exam for four hours would be challenging after finishing a three-hour class at 3:30 p.m.

However, he didn't let my words come out. He cut me off after my first sentence, giving me an outraged look, and said, "I know you have classes on Fridays, and they end at 3:30."

I froze due to his gesture and tone. He took a step toward me. I remained completely frozen.

"I am trying to find a solution here," he said, mixed with other remarks I can't quite recall.

His furious tone and a gesture directed at me left me utterly stunned. It was as if he were saying, *How dare you speak? I'm the one making the decisions here. You're not supposed to be in this class, let alone express your viewpoint.*

He then rolled his eyes and moved away from me. The discussion continued as other students shared their opinions.

He calmly engaged with each of them and, at one point, even made a joke about not being a fan of exams while he was in law school himself. Throughout this time, I remained frozen in my seat, unable to look at him or the other students, struggling to process what had just happened.

For the next hour, I found it impossible to concentrate on what was being taught. My head remained lowered, my hands and feet shaking. I swallowed the lump in my throat and tried to breathe through my painful chest. Later, I realized I was experiencing a panic attack in those moments.

All the while, I blamed myself and repeated phrases like *You're overreacting*, *He didn't mean anything by it*, and *It's just his way of speaking.*

I was finding excuses for his actions.

The class ended, and right away, one of my classmates called out to me from the back seat.

"I noticed how the professor talked to you. It was not okay, and I am sorry," she said.

I couldn't even find the words to respond; I simply burst into tears. It wasn't me overreacting—someone else had recognized what had happened. Later, another classmate approached me, expressing that he had noticed how I was treated during the class.

"He doesn't seem to like us," he remarked. I looked at him; he was a person of color like me. "That's why I try not to speak up in the class," he continued.

I contacted the university deans to address the situation. I explained to them that I no longer felt comfortable speaking up in that class due to the incident. I respectfully asked to be transferred to a different course. This occurred during the third week of the semester, and making up for the missed material was still feasible.

A week later, I received a response from the deans, who asserted that they perceived the situation as a misunderstanding, echoing the stance of the pharmacist and numerous others. They conveyed their reluctance to establish a precedent where students could change courses in response to similar incidents.

They proposed a meeting involving the professor, me, and one of the assistant deans to address the incident. To me, this offer was far from an equitable solution. I pictured myself in that room, facing people of power who would try to downplay the situation.

I told the deans that I had sacrificed so much to be in law school, and my grades and performance were important to me. I didn't want to jeopardize them by confronting the professor, who still held the power to grade me.

"It's a misunderstanding, you'll see in the meeting," they said.

At this point, I had to make a choice: engage in a potentially futile conversation or remain silent to protect my mental health. I chose the latter path because I couldn't envision having equal power and rights in such a discussion. One side was me, a minority woman of color, and the other side was a white man with privileges. The deans, who were supposed to be neutral, had already aligned themselves with their "misunderstanding" justifications. I didn't want to get caught up in their pattern of *we acknowledge you, but you've misunderstood.*

How should I participate in a meeting where I'd need to convince others that my experience of discrimination, based on my race, skin color, accent, and minority status in the class, was valid, especially when they didn't believe me beforehand? I kept asking myself.

I felt disappointed.

"I came to law school to strengthen my voice, but now I just feel so powerless," I confided in a friend.

"You're far from powerless. You spoke up, but the school let you down. It's not your fault, it's on them," she reassured me.

When I declined the meeting, the school seemed content to brush the issue aside as if it had never occurred.

I succeeded in finishing that class with an A. I was resolute in my determination not to let the professor negatively influence my education or dampen my enthusiasm for one of my favorite law subjects. Nonetheless, I always felt uneasy in his presence. I avoided sitting in the front row, and if I glimpsed him in the hallway, I would change my route to sidestep any chance of a face-to-face encounter. I experienced more panic attacks a few weeks after the incident, and I had to seek medical assistance to control them.

A few months later, another professor—again a white man—threw a marker towards me to signal that the break had ended, and I needed to return to my seat.

I was standing in front of the class, talking with a friend seated in the front row. Students continued talking, the room still loud, when, a sharp *bang* sound behind me drew the entire class's attention. I looked behind me and noticed a marker on the floor, then shifted my gaze back to the professor. He was laughing, seemingly having made a humorous gesture.

In haste, I returned to my seat amidst the ongoing commotion in the classroom while the professor said, with a sneer, "It didn't hit her."

"It's okay," I whispered, although the situation was anything but okay.

Throughout the journey back home, I struggled to convince myself that it was just a joke. I was again in denial mode, trying to find an excuse.

"There were other ways he could have gotten your attention—he could have raised his voice, walked over, slapped the table, or even yelled loudly. But throwing a marker was not appropriate," one of my classmates told me the next day when I told her about the incident.

"He wouldn't have thrown a marker at me," she continued.

I looked at her. She was right. He would not dare to throw a marker at a forty-year-old white woman. Yet he did throw it at me, much like Mrs. H, the pharmacy customer, and the other professor. To all of them, I appeared to be the weakest person in the room, an easy target, someone upon whom they could exercise their authority to undermine and belittle.

The truth is, being a minority on various fronts makes me an easy target. Instead of holding those responsible accountable, society often puts weight on people like me to endure and tolerate this unfair treatment. Our vulnerabilities are twisted to manipulate us, often with excuses like us not understanding the culture, being too sensitive, or not getting the jokes. These manipulative explanations are used to quiet us down, and sadly, they tend to work.

This time, I decided not to report the incident to the deans' office.

*

Racial discrimination is complex, multi-dimensional, and often concealed beneath layers. People often reject its existence because it isn't easily observable. Yet it's real. The fact that the wounds from these experiences aren't outwardly visible doesn't diminish their importance.

I still carry a piece of those days from the grocery store with me, even as the years have turned into a decade. I was silent in the grocery store and was silenced at the law school. I was hurt when the pharmacist would not tell that customer that they would not offer him any services due to his behavior, and I was even more hurt when the deans would not believe me, would not confront the professor, and would not transfer me into another class to protect me.

The ache in my heart serves as a reminder—not just of the pain, but of the resilience that has been forged in its wake. It's a reminder that our struggles, even those hidden from the world, are valid and deserving of recognition. In a society that often prefers the comfort of ignorance, our stories have the power to peel back those layers and expose the truth that lies beneath.

QUEEN OF THE MOUNTAINS*

I left Iran with two suitcases and a backpack, hastily packed the essentials. The rest of my belongings stayed behind in my room at my parents' home in Tehran. When I left, I was angry. I said I would never come back, but beneath the anger, there was a quiet hope—a belief that one day, I'd return. Maybe not to stay, but at least to visit. I told myself I'd go back each year, reclaim my belongings bit by bit, and maybe bring them to Canada.

For a time, my mother held onto that hope for me. She kept my room intact as if I might walk back through the door at any moment. But before long, my father was arrested. And with that, everything changed. The hope I had buried under anger began to fade, worn down by the realities of exile. My advocacy for him only widened the distance between me and the life I'd left behind, turning the possibility of return into something more dangerous, even impossible. I had become a threat to the Iranian regime, someone who challenged their authority. If I returned, I would face persecution and imprisonment.

My mother then began urging me to let go. "There's no point in keeping your things," she'd say. "Give them to someone who can use them." Her words were logical, but each suggestion chipped away at the fragile thread I still held onto.

She went after my clothes first. Every day she would pull out a pile from my wardrobe, take some photos, and send them to me with messages like, "This green dress is too tight

* An excerpt of this story was published in The Humber Literary Review, 2023.

for you. You remember you couldn't move your arms?"

I had bought the dress for my cousin's wedding. I liked everything about the dress, but it did feel tight beneath my armpits, meaning I couldn't reach above shoulder level. Despite my mother's warning, I wore it to the wedding, where I'd carefully move my hands when I was dancing. Everything was fine until the Kurdish dance began. In every Iranian wedding, the Kurdish dance is the spotlight of the ceremony. It's the dance that everyone, from kids to seniors, can join, standing shoulder to shoulder in a circle, locking elbows and grabbing each other's hands, then jumping and swinging hands up and down, up and down, all together.

The second I joined the circle, I remembered my dress problem, but it was too late. As soon as my hands shot above my shoulder, I heard the awful sound of fabric tearing. My aunt on the other side of the circle was moving her eyebrows up and down, pointing at my armpit. I nodded my head, meaning that I knew, but there was no way to escape.

The rest of the night I sat at my table, arms close to my body. I tried to avoid looking at my mother's *I-told-you-not-to-wear-this-dress* face. She later fixed the dress. Still, I never danced in it again.

"I'm going to donate all these winter clothes. You said they are useless there," she texted. That message came with pictures of all my colourful pullovers, jackets, and coats. I didn't resist. She was right. The definition of *winter clothes* changed for me once I experienced winter in Canada. None of the clothes and boots I had brought from Iran were helpful. I had to buy real winter clothes just to survive freezing. Still, each piece back home held a special memory for me. I wore those clothes at weddings, to birthday parties, on my first dates, and to graduation ceremonies.

Even so, my mother was right: "What is the point of keeping them when you can't wear them?"

A year later, though, she surprised me with a patchwork coat, fashioned from my most memorable clothes. Assembling the fabrics in an artistic way, she had sewn a coat for me. A coat that carried all those memories.

After clothes, it was my books. Floor-to-ceiling bookshelves lined one wall of my room, filled with books I had been gifted or had bought. The books were not only a treasury of knowledge; they were attached to memories of learning, laughing, and crying as I'd read them. These memories made it doubly hard to say goodbye. My mother gave the books away to a library in a village. "Imagine how many girls could have access to what you had?" she wrote. She knew I could not say no to a women-empowering plan.

Clothes and shoes gone, bookshelves bare, childhood toys gone, too; my desk and bed were the last to go. Finally, my mother had the space she needed. She transformed my room into the sewing room she'd always wished for.

In our small apartment, no one had their own space. All the rooms were multifunctional. There was a freezer in my bedroom and an extra fridge on the balcony that protruded from my room. This arrangement meant I could never have the privacy I wanted. I would lie in my bed with a friend, our legs up against the wall as we talked about the boys we had crushes on whom we met every day on the way to school. Suddenly my father would enter the room to get out to the balcony. Without a word, he would place the fruits and vegetables he had just bought in the fridge. In the middle of my concentrating on a math problem, my mom would come to grab meat or vegetables from the freezer. Most of the time, she couldn't find them, so she'd start digging around the drawers, and the freezer alarm would go off until my mother finally closed the door. By the time she'd leave my room, I'd have lost focus on my studies.

My brother had it even worse with my mother's sewing

machine and the ironing table in the corner of his room. For me, people would come to put or grab things and leave. But for him, people would come and stay to finish their work. No one treated a space as someone's room, or thought of privacy, or thought to ask permission. No one apologized for intruding. We all accepted that we had to share our space, together.

In our living room, which functioned as a dining room and family room, my father would use the dining table as his working desk. We'd want to watch TV, but my father was working or having a meeting. We'd want to eat, but his stuff was all over the table. It was total chaos when we had a party.

I still don't know why my parents liked to hold such gatherings in that small apartment. Sometimes they invited fifty people, and with not enough furniture, everyone would sit on the floor. I would go around offering tea, pastries, and fruits, carefully stepping so as not to crush anyone's hand or foot. Serving dinner was another story. My mother would put the pots on the kitchen floor, where, with the help of other guests, people would fill their plates. I would start piling more plates on the dining table, but even before we would finish setting all the stuff out, most of the guests were already full. Then it was time to bring back the dirty dishes to the kitchen and stack them on the floor to wash the next morning.

When my brother left home, my mother transformed his room into an office for my father right away. "No more writings and books on the dining table," she said. When I left, she did the same for herself. This *let everything go and make a fresh start* agenda was not just for making space. It was also my mother's response to living with our absence. Now, she was looking at a sewing room and an office instead of her children's rooms. Without our belongings, it was easier for her not to visualize memories.

Still, there is one thing in the corner of that sewing room that belongs to me. My mother never tried to get rid of it, at least not until the Covid-19 pandemic.

"I think its tires are going to be rotten soon," she texted me. She sent this message with a photo of my bike leaning against the wall. By this time, my mother was sure I wouldn't be back home. Maybe it was time to talk about the last item left in what had been my bedroom.

"Maman, if you just spin the wheels more often, nothing will happen to them," I said.

*

Growing up in Iran, I had to follow too many dos and don'ts dictated by law, religion, society, and culture. Laws written and unwritten. Especially for girls, there were more and more bans, more nos than you can imagine. One of those many taboos was riding a bike in public.

Boys and girls as kids can have bikes; it's when girls step into adolescence that most parents stop buying them bicycles. Adolescent boys go to the streets and play with their bikes. Adolescent girls, it is thought, should stay home and watch street life through the windows. Sometimes these girls sneak the use of their brothers' bikes. Some of my friends did that. Still, having one of their own would be a big no.

In our family, it was vice versa. My brother was not into cycling. I was the one who loved spending time outside. I was lucky to have open-minded parents in that society. They were always worried, but they never said no to me.

I didn't grow up in a sports-oriented family. Mountain climbing was the only physical activity I would do with my parents, on weekends since I was six. They would pack breakfast, and we would head to Shirpala or Kolakchal Mountain in north of Tehran.

On the way towards the peak, we would have our breakfast. Mohammad and I would run around to collect wood sticks and watch carefully as my father set a fire. He would pour spring water into our sooty steel kettle and place it over the fire until it boiled. Then he would add a full spoon of tea leaves and put the kettle aside, off the fire, on the wood ashes to brew. The fire infused everything around us with its smoky aroma, and the tea was no exception. Afterward, we would eat our breakfast, bread and cheese, along with the smoky tea.

I eagerly anticipated our weekly mountain adventures. However, as I grew older, I began to sense a freedom in the mountains that I couldn't find elsewhere. It was as if, once a week, we could escape the constraints of the city.

Women wore different clothes from the typical street attire; their scarves were loose or slipped off their hair entirely. They would even remove their obligatory manteau and climb in T-shirts and pants. Boys and girls hiked hand in hand, and sometimes I would witness them kissing without fear of intervention by the morality police. People would carry their cassette players and play forbidden music as we ascended the mountain.

The absence of policing, particularly of women, made me feel equal to my brother in the mountains. However, I lost this opportunity when I was twelve due to my father's knee pain and my mother's heart issues, which forced them to quit climbing.

The enduring effect of those mountain climbs made my teenage self think that being athletic was how I could demonstrate that I was just as capable as the boys. So, I took cycling seriously, as it was the only option available to me. But beyond that, I also became a passionate sports fan.

I'd spend hours glued to the TV, initially as a football fan, but eventually, freestyle wrestling became my true love. The peak of my obsession came in 1998, when the World Wrestling Championships came to Tehran. I practically lived in front of the television those days, not only soaking in the action but also interpreting the matches for my parents and anyone else who happened to be at our house.

"The shoulder was too high, and he couldn't pin down and control his opponent's hips," I would say, explaining why a wrestler's actions had failed.

"No, no, look, he needs to use his free hand to reach the remaining ankle and collect," I would say, giving my opinions on what the wrestlers should do.

I longed to be part of the action, to stand in the arena among passionate fans, shouting my heart out and supporting the Iran team. The envy would grip me whenever the entire stadium erupted into Mexican waves. "I should be there," I would plead with my parents. I knew it was a forbidden dream, as women were barred from attending stadium events. My parents would give me a bitter smile without saying anything. They had no power to grant their daughter's wish. Maybe that's why they never opposed my cycling.

As a teenager, I passed my summers by cycling for hours in the streets of Tehran. In loose jogging clothes and a cap, I would look like a boy, and no one would be suspicious. At the time, I went to a prestigious private high school with restrictive Islamic rules, like many schools of its kind. In addition to wearing a scarf and uniform, which is mandatory in Iran, I had to wear a black chador—a full-body-length fabric. So, imagine if someone from school found out about me riding a bike like that in the street. I would have been expelled.

Still, I found so much joy and freedom in my cycling, I barely cared about what it could do to my education and future.

I was sixteen when my bike broke. I tried to repair it for a week, but all attempts were unsuccessful. My father noticed my distress.

"It's time to buy a new one," he said.

I had never been in a bicycle shop before. I'd inherited my previous bike and the one before that from my cousins. It was always my brother who would get the new bike, and I would use his when he'd outgrown it. I had never had a brand-new bike, one of my very own. I couldn't imagine having one now.

Stepping into the fancy shop that my father took me to was like being in bicycle la-la land. I walked the rows, inhaling the smell of new rubber. I looked at the bikes and their features while the owner gave his lengthy speech about different Iranian brands' bikes, promoting their qualities.

"Do you have something better?" my father interrupted the owner. "I mean, which one is your best bike?"

The owner paused for a second, as if hesitating to say something. He looked at me, then at my father; then he pointed to a bike hanging from the ceiling at the far end of the shop.

"It is expensive, though," the owner cautioned. He might have thought that it was a waste of money to buy an expensive bike for a girl.

"It's okay," my father said. "Can you bring it down?" From his tone, I could tell he didn't like the owner's attitude.

The owner reluctantly retrieved the bike and handed it to my father, who passed it to me and asked, "Do you like it?"

I nodded without saying a word. I touched the body of the bike—so smooth, with no rough welding marks like my previous bikes. The silver frame, which faded into pink in some parts, was so neat and shiny. There was a place for holding a water bottle, and the bike had gears. I had never ridden a bike with gears. It was a dream bike for me, something beyond my expectations.

My father bought the French-built Peugeot bicycle. It cost him a third of his monthly salary. That surprised me. The father I knew was always going on about supporting Iranian-made products, and yet he had just bought me a foreign-brand bike. He had made an exception and gone against his beliefs because he knew that cycling was important to me. I already had so many obstacles ahead of me; before I could pursue my dream of becoming a professional cyclist, he wanted to do what he could by giving me the best bike I could ever wish for.

I was lucky. He and I shared the same feelings about cycling. Cycling for us was more than sport or entertainment. It was a tool propelling us to freedom—the freedom that we didn't have, but that we would never, ever give up on.

My father grew up in a remote village where the nearest school was ten kilometers away. The long trek discouraged most children in the area, including his own siblings, from pursuing their education beyond the basics. But my father was different. Even as a young boy, his curiosity demanded answers, and he saw school as the only place to find them.

Determined to make the journey easier, he asked my grandfather for a bicycle. For a villager, a bike was an expensive luxury, and my grandfather dismissed the idea outright. But my father began a hunger strike, holding firm until my grandfather relented and bought the bike. That bicycle became more than a means of travel. It carried him from his village to some of the most prestigious universities in the world.

*

My own dreams expanded thanks to possessing that French silver-pinkish bike. I soon wanted to become a cycling champion.

I would watch Tour de France for hours on our satellite TV and imagine myself on the road, cycling from one city to another. My favorite part was the mountain stages, where the leader gets the red polka-dot jersey and is named as King of the Mountains. I would watch all the stages with envy and ask myself, *Is it possible that I could ride a bicycle professionally one day?*

The summer that I turned eighteen, I was determined to find the answer to my question. Every day for a month, I went to the Cycling Federation and even to the National Olympic Committee to talk with authorities. As I expected, most of the time I would face closed doors. They ignored or rejected me and even humiliated me.

"What are you doing here? This is a men's place," a doorman at the Cycling Federation told me the first day I showed up. I passed through the gate and got these responses:

"What? Women cycling? Impossible."

"Are you joking? I don't have time to listen to your nonsense."

"Do you think here is Paris or New York?"

"You are like my daughter. The best thing for you is studying now. Don't confuse yourself with this stuff."

Women cycling was a taboo, and no one wanted to talk about it, let alone break it. I wrote my personal story about riding a bike in Tehran's streets and all my attempts at creating a women's cycling team. I sent my story to many newspapers. None of them published it. I didn't have the power to change the system. Still, as my grandmother would say: "Begin to weave and God will give the thread."

Through these activities, I got in touch with other girls and boys who also thought women should have the right to ride a bicycle.

When I was nineteen, we created our team and took our first cycling trip. It was not normal—and also not legal—for a group of boys and girls to travel together, let alone go backpacking on their bikes.

On the second or third day, close to sunset, I was struggling to cycle up a hill. I stood on the pedals to take full advantage of my body weight and apply more force. With each pedal, I breathed deeply. Sweat was running down my forehead and dripping into my eyes, which burned with sunscreen. I wiped my sweat with my forearm. Raising my head to take a deep breath, I saw an absolutely brilliant orange and red sun go down, right behind the mountain. There, in front of me, the sun's rays paled and slowly disappeared. *This is it*, I thought to myself. *I am Queen of the Mountains.* I felt like a champion, with no need for competition, a cheering crowd, or a polka-dot jersey.

After that, I took many road trips. Still in Iran, still on

my bike, I had my fears, worries, and difficulties, but most of the time I would enjoy pedaling and visiting different places. People would open their houses and offer me their food and local treats. I would sleep in the schools and mosques in the villages, where I would almost always be welcomed, praised, and encouraged.

People know what is right and wrong beyond the rules.

"Look, Maman! She is a girl," little girls would shout, pointing at me while I passed through their cities and villages. What they were seeing was a possibility: *If she can do it, I can do it too.*

*

I rarely get attached to things. Life has taught me to let go, especially after immigrating to Canada, where I learned the hard truth that nothing is permanent. I've lost loved ones, my home, and even fragments of my identity. By most measures, holding onto an old, worn-out bike didn't make much sense.

Yet the bike tucked away in the corner of my mother's sewing room isn't just any bike. It's a symbol of resistance, a reminder of the battles I fought and the courage it took to keep going, no matter the odds. It also carries a quiet hope: that one day, I might return and ride it again.

When my mother suggested letting it go, something inside me sank. It felt like severing the last fragile thread that connected me to the possibility of return. I couldn't let it go. I needed to keep that glimmer alive, however faint. And so, the bike stayed—a silent witness to my longing and to the battles I thought I had left behind.

Then came September 2022.

Mahsa Amini, a twenty-two-year-old woman, was tragically assaulted by Iran's morality police for allegedly wearing her hijab too loosely, an incident that led to her death. Her passing sparked outrage, becoming a rallying cry for change.

Massive protests erupted, led predominantly by women who sent a powerful message: *Enough is enough.* In acts of defiance and solidarity, women cut their hair, removed their scarves, and set them ablaze, their voices echoing in the streets as they rejected the control imposed upon them.

Many have attempted to downplay this uprising, framing it solely as a protest against compulsory hijab. However, it runs far deeper than what meets the eye. It was a protest against the entrenched and systematic gender discrimination that has plagued Iran for decades, a discrimination that predates even the Islamic revolution. It was a fight for *women* who are consistently censored in society, for the *lives* they cannot determine for themselves, and for the *freedoms* that have been violated and stripped away. That's why "*Zan, Zendegi, Azadi*"—"Woman, life, freedom"—was chosen as the slogan of this revolutionary movement.

Even women who had worn the hijab as their personal choice joined the movement. My mother, at seventy-three, was one of them. She would walk slowly through the streets, leaning on her cane, removing her white scarf, and chanting, "*Zan, Zendegi, Azadi.*"

"It's dangerous, Maman. You can't escape if they raid the protest," I warned her during one of our phone calls. But I already knew her response.

"I have lived my life," she said. "I am ready to sacrifice the rest for the freedom of the children of this land."

Women across Iran turned their streets into battlegrounds, using their voices, their courage, and even their bodies in the fight for a better future. Their resistance ignited a wave of hope that spread far beyond the borders. Iranians in diaspora organized rallies in solidarity with the women of Iran, echoing their voices.

In October, I joined one of the largest rallies in Toronto, marching alongside fifty thousand others. Together with two friends, we carried three large signs, each bearing one word of the movement's defining slogan: "Woman, Life, Freedom." I had the "Freedom" sign, which I had attached it to a rope and hung around my neck so my hands were free to clap and chant with the crowd. It swayed as I walked, a constant reminder of the message I carried—not just on the sign, but in my heart.

One group would call, "Say her name," and we would reply, "Mahsa Amini."

"Say her name!"

"Mahsa Amini."

"Say her name!"

"Mahsa Amini."

We repeated it over and over, tireless and unwavering, as if invoking her name kept her spirit alive and reminded us that we had had enough—enough of women being killed for their beliefs, their choices, their very existence.

At some point, the amplifiers all around us began to play the song "Baraye" ("For") by Shervin Hajipour, which had become the anthem of this movement. The song is a mosaic of hopes and grievances, drawn from messages shared by Iranians on social media about why they protest. As the familiar melody filled the air, the crowd joined in, singing together:

"For dancing in the streets freely,
For our fear of kissing loved ones,
For my sister, your sister, our sisters,

For this compulsory Heaven,
For elites in prison,
For the feeling of peace,
For sunrise after long dark nights,
For sedative and insomnia pills"

And then came the line that always shattered me, leaving

tears streaming down my face: "*For the girl who wished to be born as a boy.*"

That girl was me—a girl who would ride her bike through the streets, knowing it wasn't allowed, knowing the rules said she couldn't, that she shouldn't. Each ride was my silent act of rebellion, my refusal to be still. But for years, I'd thought, *If only I were a boy, everything would be easier.*

I came home from the rally that day with a new understanding of hope. It isn't always a blazing fire. Sometimes it's a quiet ember, lying dormant, waiting for the right moment to be reignited. The fight I had left behind hadn't ended—it had evolved. The hope I thought had faded was never truly lost. It had been there all along, waiting, like my bike, for the right moment to be reclaimed.

My bike still stands in the corner of my mother's sewing room. She has decorated it with two baskets, one on the front and one on the back, each brimming with pink and red geraniums.

THE FINAL GOODBYE

My father and I took the last photo together in Iran at the airport. The image is blurry. My mother's hands were shaking as she captured the last frame of us together. My father has his arm around my shoulder, leaning toward me with a smile. My green scarf loosely drapes over my hair. My usual wide smile is absent, replaced by a pale one. My broken eyeglasses sit crooked on my face—I didn't have time to replace them after the raid. My eyes look tired, smaller than usual, with no shine.

For the past decade, this blurry photo has stayed on my phone. I wouldn't say I like looking at old photos, and I haven't done so in the last ten years. But this one is different. It captured my final goodbye to my parents—one smiling and hugging me in front of the camera and the other shaking behind it. The gray floor, white airport walls in the background, and the black bolted benches where we sit mark the last station before leaving home. My crooked eyeglasses and blurry image reflect my broken heart and the uncertain path ahead.

As the years passed, the more I looked at the photo, the more I have realized how my destiny was captured within it.

Nearly a decade after our farewell at the Tehran airport, I reunited with my father in Istanbul. The authorities had finally lifted his travel ban and granted him a passport, allowing him to leave Iran at last.

I spent a week with my parents in Istanbul, trying to do ordinary things I had missed for so long. We cooked together, went shopping, took walks, and enjoyed long chats over afternoon tea. During any activity, I would observe them in detail, searching for familiarity.

I would stand by the kitchen door and watch my mother prepare meals. She would fry onions on a low flame, then add turmeric just before they turned a crispy golden color—a habit of hers. I would serve her tea and observe how she poured just the right amount of milk into it. I would watch my father prepare the salad by cutting lettuce into large pieces and slicing tomatoes and cucumbers thickly, as he used to do, and how, during lunch and dinner, he tore a piece of bread from the loaf, using it to scoop up yogurt from the bowl.

One night, I asked my father to make me an omelet. "I have a PhD in omelet-making," he would always boast, especially when trying to convince unexpected guests to stay and eat with us. His omelet was the only dish I preferred over my mother's cooking. I stood beside him, watching as he prepared it. First, he sautéed the chopped onions, then added thick chunks of tomato to the pan. He waited for the moisture to evaporate before cracking in the eggs, stirring everything together. Finally, he sprinkled a pinch of dried basil on top—just as I remembered.

But in each familiar gesture, something was missing—as if the parents I once knew had subtly changed. Their sleep routines, the foods they once loved but no longer ate, the slowness in completing tasks, the new medications they took, the way they spoke to me, the concerns that once preoccupied them but seemed to no longer matter—all of it felt different now.

One day, as we walked down the street, I noticed their aging figures ahead of me. They seemed petite, as if they had shrunk, with a slight hunch in their backs. My mother held the handle of a cane in her right hand, wearing a white glove to protect her psoriasis scars and wounds from the pressure of the cane. With each step, she moved the cane first, testing the ground before rolling her left foot, then her right. My father walked ahead of her, his torso leaning slightly to the right. His steps were steady, yet something about his movement felt unbalanced. They looked unfamiliar to me. *Who are they?* I felt a deep sense of distance from the image I saw.

One week wasn't enough to reconnect, to truly understand who my parents had become. It wasn't enough to reclaim what I had lost or make up for what I had missed. I didn't want to return to Canada. I was willing to give up everything to stay with them. But once again, the time to leave them arrived.

My flight was a few days before theirs, on a quiet Saturday morning. Baghdad Avenue was empty at that hour, with only a yellow taxi waiting to take me to the airport. The sun bathed the street in a soft glow. A gentle breeze caressed my face, carrying with it the salty scent of the Marmara Sea.

I hugged my father first. He pulled me close, holding me tightly for what felt like a long minute. His rough, unshaven cheek brushed against me as he kissed me. Behind that roughness, I could feel his face trembling as he clenched his teeth to hide it. Then, my mother embraced me. The reality of leaving them again hit me at that moment, and I burst into tears. I didn't want her to let go. I wanted to be a child in her arms once more, carried wherever she went. I didn't care that I was a forty-year-old adult woman—I wept like a baby in her embrace. She smelled of jasmine blossoms, just as she always had. It was the scent I remembered, the scent I had longed for.

"Tyranny won't last forever, have hope," my mother whispered. Gently, she released me, her gaze locking with mine. "We will be together again one day. But now, it's time to go," she said, her hazel eyes shimmering with unshed tears.

I still don't know where or how she finds the strength to let go of her child every time, but it is that very strength that keeps me going, helping me bear this unbearable separation.

Gathering the shattered pieces of myself, I sat in the taxi. As the car began to move, I couldn't take my eyes off the fragile figures of my parents standing in the street, smiling and waving goodbye. I sobbed like a child being torn away from her parents by force.

"Who were they?" The taxi driver's voice broke the heaviness in the car.

"My parents," I replied, holding back my tears.

"Where do you go?" he asked.

"Canada," I said.

"My son lives in Canada, too," he said. There was something familiar in the tone of his voice and the way he glanced at me in the mirror. He knew the pain of leaving. We talked for an hour on the way to the airport, using his basic English and my basic Turkish. He comforted me like a father. He tried to distract me from the pain I was enduring, but the pain had captured my entire body, like metastatic cancer without a cure.

I pondered many questions at the airport and throughout my eleven-hour flight to Toronto. *After a decade of living in Canada, why does this move still feel temporary?* I knew I couldn't return anytime soon. After all the advocacy I did for my father, I am now a target for Iranian authorities. I could be accused of "spreading propaganda against the State"—a common charge against activists in Iran—and face imprisonment. I am technically living in exile. *But why I don't accept Canada as my home? Why do I feel displaced?*

I had carried these questions within me for so long, and I felt it was finally time to confront them.

When I left Iran, I was angry and hurt. I just wanted to escape all those pains. Sometimes, I wondered if I had cursed my home that day in the bathroom after the raid when I stomped and yelled, "I hate you." Or when I refused to let my mother throw water behind me—a traditional Iranian custom meant to ensure the safe return of travelers. "I don't want to return," I told her, though I didn't mean it. I hadn't properly said goodbye to many friends and family as planned. The raid had ruined my farewell gatherings, disrupted my focus on preparing to leave, and even broken the promise I had made to myself years earlier.

*

I was around twenty at the time. After an argument with my mother, I left home without saying goodbye. I don't remember the details of the argument, but it was probably something trivial, like many disputes young people have with their parents. I slammed the door and walked out.

An hour later, I received a call from a man using my mother's phone. He told me that the bus she was on had been in an accident, and she had fallen from her seat.

"She can't move," he said. "We are waiting for an ambulance," he added. My mother's voice, moaning from the pain, echoed in my ear.

I asked where they were located. It wasn't far from where I was, so I took a taxi. However, as we neared the area—within two kilometers—the traffic became so heavy that we were stuck, likely due to the accident. I got out of the taxi and ran the rest of the way. One thought consumed me as I ran down Valiasr Street: *I didn't say goodbye to Maman.*

I wasn't a runner, and after a few minutes, I could barely catch my breath, but I couldn't stop. I was terrified that something might happen to my mother before I had a chance to say goodbye. My legs felt like they weren't my own that day. My body shook as I ran, and I feared I might collapse at any moment, but I couldn't make my legs stop. "I have to see Maman before it's too late," I kept repeating.

When I arrived at the accident scene, I saw the ambulance pulling away. I could barely breathe and started coughing. The man I had spoken with earlier approached and asked if I was okay.

"My mother," I managed to gasp, pointing to the ambulance

growing smaller in the distance. I choked on my coughing and collapsed to my knees in the street, drained of all strength.

"Don't worry, she's fine," he said, trying to comfort me.

We were fortunate that day. My mother didn't have severe injuries and was released from the emergency room a couple of hours later. However, after that incident, I made the promise to say goodbye properly to my loved ones. I never wanted to experience that feeling again. It's even become a rule in my marriage: no matter how we feel or how rushed we are, Aydin and I make it a point to say goodbye and share a hug whenever we leave home.

The only time I'd broken my promise since the accident was when I left Iran. Unable to say goodbye, I felt like I had been on a temporary journey and had longed to return ever since. I had been running to reclaim what I had left behind and offer my belated goodbyes. But this temporary journey seemed never-ending. It felt like I was on a one-way road, always moving forward, yet I searched for a turn signal to make a U-turn at every intersection, only to find none.

Like many immigrants, I have lost many things—including my parents. They are still alive, but no longer present in my new life. The grief inside me kept me from moving forward, as if I were in a state of constant mourning. My immigrant friends cope with their loss in different ways. Some choose to forget, burying the past to ignore what they have lost and focusing solely on what they have in their new lands. They even stop speaking their mother tongues with their children, severing the last connection to their homeland. Some others are trapped in nostalgia, constantly sighing and regretting what they left behind. They remain unhappy and unsatisfied no matter what they achieve or accomplish here.

I had tried both paths, and neither helped me. I wanted to cherish what I had in Canada while honoring what I had in the past. I didn't want to forget; I wanted to remember—

that's why I write. Yet I didn't want to be trapped in the past either, imprisoned by memories that could no longer be. What I needed was to carry both the past and the present in harmony. And the only way to do that was to say my belated goodbyes to everything I had lost. The goodbye wasn't a way to forget, but a way to acknowledge my memories, accept my losses, and learn to live peacefully with them.

"I need closure," I told Aydin back in Canada.

"We could have a ceremony, if that would help," Aydin suggested. "I can put together all the traditional mourning rituals—bouquets, framed photos, dates, halva, whatever you want."

I couldn't help but smile. "How about death announcements, like the one we did for Asad?"

A laugh escaped both of us as the memory from years ago resurfaced.

*

As a freshman, everything except the lessons was still novel and exciting at the University of Tehran. A few months ago, my only dream had been to get good scores on the entrance exam and pass through the university gates. I hadn't been accepted into medical school as I had planned, but the large campus, with its many social and political activities and events, fascinated me more than the feeling of rejection. Although I was still living at my parents' house, being on campus gave me a sense of independence. It was a new world for me, and I wanted to try new things and explore it all.

Most of the professors at the university were friendly. They showed great patience with us, a class of fifty-two freshmen who were still trying to adjust to the difference between high school and university life. It wasn't just about the lessons in the classroom; they made an effort to connect with us, cracking jokes, engaging in chats on various subjects, and providing guidance as we navigated this new phase of life.

Dr. Sheikh, our math professor, stood out as an exception. She was the youngest among the professors, having just graduated with her PhD. From the beginning, she adopted a serious and tough demeanor, which made her seem less approachable compared to others. Reflecting on it now, I realize she had no choice but to adopt that approach to maintain control over a class full of mischievous eighteen-year-old students. At the time, however, we struggled to connect with her approach, and as classes went on, our resentment towards her grew.

Dr. Sheikh was tall and slim. She always wore high heels which wasn't common on our campus at all. This made her taller than necessary. When she walked in front of the class on the stage and wrote on the board, I was always distracted by the sounds of her shoes: *click, clack—click, clack*. She also wore a black chador over her uniform and scarf. One hand was always holding the chador under her chin to keep it from falling, while the other hand wrote on the board. I admired how she could walk and teach for an hour and a half in high heels while also managing her chador.

In the second month at university, we decided to play a prank on her. We wanted to somehow break her stern demeanor. The idea started with the boys in the class and soon spread to the girls. At first, we joked about it, but then it became more serious.

The plan was simple: We were going to fake the death of one of us. We just needed to choose the right person and wait for the perfect moment.

"How about Asad?" one of the boys suggested during one of our secret meetings.

Unsurprisingly, everyone agreed. Asad was one of the smartest in the class. He would solve the toughest math problems and was chosen as a team lead by our professor. In short, he was her favorite.

We needed a photo of Asad for his death announcement. Back

then, there was no social media to access a variety of photos, so the boys discreetly took his student ID card from his bag, scanned the photo, and managed to return it without him noticing.

Aydin and another classmate designed the death announcement with great care. It began with a religious quote from the Quran at the top of the page: "*Inna Lillahi wa inna ilaihi raji'un*," which translates to: "We belong to Allah and to Him shall we return." In the middle of the page, we placed Asad's photo, and beneath it, his name was written in bold. The announcement continued as follows:

"It is with our deepest sorrow that we inform you of the passing of our beloved friend and classmate on October 11, 2002. A memorial will be held on October 18 at 3 p.m. at Behesht-e-Zahra to honor his memory. Your presence will be a great support to his family and friends. A bus will be available for transportation to Behesht-e Zahra from the university main gate at 1 p.m."

We wrote our last names beneath the announcement and printed a hundred copies to post around the campus.

The next step was to keep Asad away from university for a day. We initially thought to ask for his help for a fake move or painting a room. But when he told one of the boys that he had to return to his hometown for a couple of days due to a family matter, we were thrilled to finally put our plan into action.

On that fateful day, we arrived on campus early, two hours before our 9 a.m. math class. We placed the death announcement all around the chemistry faculty: on every notice board we could find; in the lunchroom, library, and labs.

In front of the classroom, we set up a table in keeping with traditional Iranian funeral customs. A framed photo of Asad, adorned with a black ribbon, was placed on the top left corner. Soft candlelight flickered on either side of the picture, casting a gentle glow over the scene. Plates of dates and halva were arranged on the top-right side, and white and red rose petals adorned the empty spaces in between. We placed a white rose bouquet on Asad's seat in the second row on the left, his usual spot.

By 9 a.m., the entire class had gathered together. We all had worn black clothes, making our fake memorial ceremony more compelling. We sat on our seats and waited for Dr. Sheikh's entrance.

We heard the sounds of high heels getting closer, *click, clack.*

"She is coming," someone whispered.

All noise ceased. It was as if we were holding our collective breath. The sound of the heels stopped just behind the door. Dr. Sheikh hesitated before entering. We had posted one of the announcements on the door, and she was reading it. Eventually, she opened the door, and I could see the shock in her eyes. The sight of the class dressed in black and the table set in front of the room "confirmed" what she had just read.

She remained silent and walked toward the board. As planned, one of the boys stood up and said, "Professor, we lost Asad, and before starting our class, we'd like to observe a minute of silence for him."

"Sure," she managed to say.

We all stood up, attempting to be still and silent. The professor's head was down, and even from eight rows away, I could see tears in her eyes. She was clearly in shock over losing a favorite student. Beside me, Fatemeh started giggling uncontrollably. I struggled to keep myself composed, and so did the others. In an effort to stifle her laughter, I gently pushed Fatemeh under the desk, and she covered her mouth to suppress any sounds, but her body trembled with amusement.

After the minute of silence, we sat back down and gazed at Dr. Sheikh, whose face was pale. One of the boys began distributing the dates and halva. He offered to her first. She took one date from the plate, and I saw how her hands were shaking.

"Today's class will be canceled," Dr. Sheikh announced

few minutes later.

We watched her walk toward the door. Just before reaching the doorway, her foot slipped, and she almost fell, but she managed to grasp the corner of the table to steady herself.

The class remained silent as we listened to the sound of her footsteps fading away down the hallway. Then, unable to contain ourselves any longer, the entire class burst into laughter.

We'd done it. We'd broken her.

Our plan, however, had unforeseen consequences. The announcement caught the attention of other professors and students throughout the faculty. One of the administrative staff members fainted upon seeing it, and everyone started asking us about how Asad passed away.

Our little plan was now beyond our control. Nevertheless, we maintained our roles until Asad returned two days later, completely unaware of what had transpired in his absence. As he stepped into the faculty, he might have received some odd looks, but when the faculty dean saw him, we were all summoned for an explanation.

In the dean's office, there wasn't enough space for all of us, so he decided to come to our class instead. Standing in front of us on the stage, he appeared bewildered, not knowing how to address the situation.

"I can't believe you made fun of your classmate's death," he expressed, clearly taken aback.

Asad was sitting in his regular seat, reading the death announcement we had placed there along with a flower bouquet just two days before.

"It's okay, sir. I find it cool," he responded.

Asad's unexpected reaction broke the tension, and we all burst into laughter, including the dean, who seemed unable to control the situation either. By end of the day, we all had to sign a written apology, acknowledging our mistake and expressing deep remorse to anyone who had been disturbed or hurt by our actions.

In the weeks that followed, Dr. Sheikh came to class without her usual high heels.

*

We went too far with that prank. We were young and naïve, with no real understanding of death and loss. Back then, I thought it was harmless to laugh at the fake ceremony for Asad's "death" because, after all, he was alive. I didn't yet understand the complexity of losing someone or something that's still alive but feels out of reach. I was unaware of the true meaning of loss.

Now, with the weight of real grief behind me, I understand the pain of absence—both the permanent loss of those who have passed and the aching distance from those still alive but no longer part of my life.

"I don't want a ceremony. What I need is to write," I told Aydin. For the past decade, writing had been my way of healing—my way of making sense of the pain—and I knew that this time, it would help me again.

I placed a blank sheet of paper in front of me and, with my fountain pen, began to write down everything I needed to say goodbye to. Days went by, and the page filled with names of people, things, and places. I am not a poet, but I started saying goodbye to each one with a poem, feeling that this final farewell should be grand. I had postponed this goodbye for so long—a decade. But it was time.

I read and reread the poem for days and weeks that followed. Sometimes I read it aloud, tears streaming down my face, shouting each word as if I were desperate to release the grief I had held for so long. Other times, I whispered it softly, like a lullaby, soothing my aching heart. The more I immersed myself in those words, the more I felt myself letting go. Even now, when a wave of deep grief consumes me, I return to my goodbye poem. I don't expect the pain of loss to completely fade, but I am learning to live with it peacefully.

I still feel displaced. I continue searching for a place to call home. Even if I never find it, I will carry all essence of home in my soul, in my heart: the smell of fresh bread, the sight of my mother's African violets and other plants, the sound of my father writing on paper with his fountain pen, the unwavering support of my brother who ate my burnt cakes and always said they were delicious, the warmth of the sun in the Lut Desert, the wind against my face while riding my bike, the hustle and bustle of Tajrish Bazaar, and so many other things.

This poem is my final *bedrood*—farewell—to all I once called home:

I left you without saying goodbye,
I struck you, I cursed you, I cried,
"I hate you, I hate you," I yelled,
But I didn't mean what I exhaled.

I blamed you for what I felt,
For all the tears that I had wept,
"I don't want to return," I declared,
But I didn't mean what I exhaled.

Bedrood, my home, my motherland,
I'm sorry that I didn't say goodbye as I planned,
Didn't hold you tight,
And left without a farewell, lost in the night.

Bedrood to walking Tehran's streets in fall rains,
Bedrood Valiasr, plane trees, and water flows in street drains,
Bedrood Shariati, *bedrood* Enghelab, *bedrood* again,
Bedrood Darband, where my childhood joys remain.

Bedrood mountainsides, those I climbed and those I didn't,
Damavand, Tochal, Alvand,
Bedrood rivers, those I explored and all those your maps record,
Karun, Aras, Arvand.

Bedrood Persian Gulf, Caspian Sea, in the south and the north,
Bedrood Lut Desert, your silence and warmth, from where I set forth.
Bedrood historic structures I adored, *qanāt*, "wind catchers," ā*b-anb*ā*r*,
Bedrood to cities explored and unexplored, Yazd, Bushehr, Chabahar.

I left you without saying goodbye,
I struck you, I cursed you, I cried,
"I hate you, I hate you," I yelled,
But I didn't mean what I exhaled.

I blamed you for what I felt,
For all the tears I had wept,
For the fears that never ended,
For the fake happiness I pretended.

For the women silenced,
For the lives ended,
For the freedoms stolen,
And the rights never given.

Bedrood, my home, my motherland,
I'm sorry that I didn't say goodbye as I planned,

Didn't hold you tight,
And left without a farewell, lost in the night.

Bedrood bakeries, *bedrood* to the scent of fresh breads,
sangaks, *taftoons*, *barbaris*,
Bedrood groceries, *bedrood* to the taste of your fruits,
Shemiran apples, sweet lemons, white mulberries.

Bedrood bazaars, *bedrood* to all the stalls,
Drapers, haberdashers, cobblers, carpet sellers, all,
Bedrood Tajrish, where I never grew bored,
Walking through your arched halls.

Bedrood my room, the walls, the silent witnesses of my delights and plight,
Bedrood bookshelves and the books, my refuge through an unjust fight,
Bedrood diaries, carrying memories that helped me flee,
Bedrood my bike, the only place I felt truly free.

I am bleeding from my heart,
For this decade of being apart,
I am captive to my longing,
Searching for my home and belonging.

From city to city, from one home to another,
I search for a place to fit in, to belong, fondly remember,
The more I try, the more I feel I'm wrong,
I am displaced, I feel lost in this sad song.

I must say goodbye to everyone and everything I left behind,
I won't forget you nor keep you trapped in my mind,
I carve your names into my heart, carry you along when

I depart,
But I must say goodbye for a new start.

Bedrood schools I studied in, *bedrood* workplaces,
Bedrood classmates, friends, colleagues,
Bedrood music classes, the instruments I clutched,
The *daf*, *setar*, and harmonica I touched.

Bedrood aunts, uncles, cousins, my heart wrenches as I recall
The tone of your voices, the shine of your eyes.
Bedrood mosques, the sound of azan, the prayers' calls,
Bedrood holy tombs, the smell of rosewater on your stones.

Bedrood Mohammad, *bedrood* brother,
My support and motivator,
My refuge and shield against all,
The only one who put me first even if he'd fall.

Bedrood Baba, *bedrood* father,
The dance of your fountain pen on paper,
The lamplight shimmering through your door at night,
The sound of flipping pages, a soothing lullaby out of sight.

Bedrood Maman, *bedrood* mother,
The African violets and all the plants you grow like no other,
The scent of jasmine in your hug, everywhere its trace,
The taste of food you craft with grace.

Bedrood Maman, *bedrood* my mentor, my best friend,
The long talks, our secrets, transcend,
The nights you caressed my back,

Soothing me when nights were black.

"Tyranny won't last," you whispered in my ears,
"Have hope," you said as you wiped away my tears.
One day, we will reunite again.
Khodahafez, goodbye, until then.

ACKNOWLEDGMENTS

I am immensely grateful to my brother, Mohammad, who believed in this book long before it existed. He read multiple drafts and, with his loving yet honest critiques, pushed me to create the best version of it.

Thank you to my cousins—Sara, for the countless hours of thoughtful conversation; Farideh, for lending her editorial eye to my earliest drafts; and Ali, for the strength of his presence.

I am especially thankful to Clare Robinson, whose insight and belief in the importance of my advocacy stories encouraged me to write openly about struggles and emotions I had long kept unspoken.

I am deeply grateful to Adam Braver, my editor, for his trust in my voice; his confidence and support gave me the strength to complete this book. I am also thankful to G.K. Darby and the entire team at the University of New Orleans Press for their dedication to amplifying silenced voices.

I am grateful to the editors, readers, and friends who read parts or the entirety of this book over the years, offering invaluable feedback and insight.

I remain forever thankful to my parents for the values they instilled in me from childhood and for all the opportunities for growth they provided along the way.

And finally, my immeasurable gratitude goes to Aydin, who has carried and lived these stories alongside me every step of the way; I could not have done this without you.

ABOUT THE AUTHOR

Maryam Rafiee immigrated to Canada in 2014 and is a lawyer based in Toronto. She is the author of *Dear Baba: A Story Through Letters.*